NOTES

Introduction

Jane Austen started writing at the age of eleven, first anarchic parodies of contemporary fiction, then longer stories that foreshadowed the novels. From about 1795 she was sketching out three full-length works; one of these, begun a year later when she was 20, about the age of her heroine, was *First Impressions*, an early version of *Pride and Prejudice*. This was offered by her father to the publisher Thomas Cadell, who declined even to see the manuscript. It was one of the worst publishing decisions in history.

Eventually printed 17 years later, when Austen was 38, *Pride and Prejudice* is the most satisfying and enjoyable of her six books – and has become probably the most successful novel in the English language.

Despite the astringency of her writing, Austen is often thought of as the mother of romance. She has made the Regency period (1811-1820), when all six novels were published, almost synonymous with modern popular notions of the romantic. Directly or indirectly, she has influenced romantic novels by authors such as Georgette Heyer and Daphne du Maurier and supermarket fodder of the sort published by Harlequin Romance and Mills and Boon.

Of all her books, though, it is *Pride and Prejudice* which comes closest to delivering the fairytale story of the ordinary girl who catches and marries a prince. The most inventive and ebullient of her works, it is also the one which closes with the heroine most in the ascendancy and least controlled by either parent or husband. Here, for the only time in Austen's novels, the romantic dream of bourgeois individualism taming aristocratic authority actually does come true.

But if, on one level, *Pride and Prejudice* is a reworking of the Cinderella story, it is a fiction of much greater depth than Austen's ironic, self-deprecating description of it as "rather too light & bright & sparkling" would suggest. "Beneath the light, bright and sparkling surface," says Edward Neill in *The Politics of Jane Austen*, "it investigates the social heart of darkness." W.H. Auden famously wrote in 1937:

> You could not shock her more than she shocks me;
> Beside her Joyce seems innocent as grass.
> It makes me most uncomfortable to see
> An English spinster of the middle-class
> Describe the amorous effects of "brass",
> Reveal so frankly and with such sobriety
> The economic basis of society.

A.A. Gill made much the same point when he described *Pride and Prejudice* in *The Sunday Times* as depicting a marketplace for "selling teenage virginity for cash and crenellations".

Other critics have gone even further. The psychologist D.W. Harding, for example, argued in a much-quoted essay, "Regulated Hatred", that what we see in *Pride and Prejudice* is a chilling playing out of the author's troubled psyche – the "caustic and subversive ironies" of the novel, said Harding, allowed Austen to survive in a world she actually detested and feared, an exercise not so much in fond satire as in "regulated hatred". Whatever Austen felt, it is certainly true that she was conscious of the tensions simmering below the surface of the world she wrote about.

The world is a limited one. By her own admission, she created a "little bit (two inches wide) of Ivory on which I work with so fine a Brush", advising her niece that "3 or 4 Families in a Country Village is the very thing to work on". And work on it she did, with an artistry which few novelists have matched. Within her deliberately selected confines, she explores, in *Pride and Prejudice*, not just what it is like to be a young girl in search of a suitable husband, but what it is to be human, brilliantly illuminating the difficulties of the individual living within society and the necessity constantly to reconcile personal needs with those of the wider world around one.

A summary of the plot

Five daughters are born to Mr and Mrs Bennet, a gentleman whose estate is entailed and must fall after his death to the nearest male relative; his wife, rather beneath him in birth and education, greatly laments the entail. Given the very few options for genteel girls, the daughters must marry well if they are to retain a decent position in society; nonetheless the two eldest and most sensible, Elizabeth and Jane, cannot imagine actually husband-hunting. Mr Bennet, a sardonic man who enjoys mocking his vulgar wife and silly younger daughters, favours Elizabeth because of her intelligence; as a result she has been given much freedom at home for her quickness in response.

The entry of four gentlemen into the Bennet society sets the plot in motion. The first is an apparently proud and disagreeable but rich and handsome man called Darcy; he accompanies his friend Bingley, who has taken a lease on a neighbouring house. At a local dance he makes a disparaging remark about Elizabeth's inadequate beauty, which she overhears, resents and mocks. Meanwhile her sister Jane and Bingley are falling in love – to Mrs Bennet's loud delight. The third male arrival is the Bennet heir, Mr Collins, an absurd clergyman impressed by the grandeur of his patroness, Lady Catherine de Burgh, who is Mr Darcy's aunt; Mr Collins intends to marry one of the Bennet daughters to compensate for the fact that he will succeed to their property. Mrs Bennet declares Jane spoken for, so his choice falls on Elizabeth, who struggles to refuse his preposterous proposal. (Shortly afterwards, her older and plain friend Charlotte, with less refined views on marriage, learns of Elizabeth's refusal and takes the rejected suitor for herself.) The fourth man is a soldier, Wickham, charming son of the estate manager of Mr Darcy's father – he movingly describes Darcy's persecution and envy of himself. He flirts with silly Lydia Bennet and more seriously engages Elizabeth's attention; she finds him attractive and plausible.

Meanwhile, despite his unfortunate first impression on her, Darcy is finding Elizabeth's wit, sparkle and bright eyes increasingly alluring. To her great surprise, when she visits Charlotte, now married to Mr Collins, he proposes marriage, at the same time declaring the struggle he has had with himself over approaching a lady with such deplorable relations. Astounded by this frankness and having learnt that Darcy had parted her sister from his friend Bingley, Elizabeth rejects him roundly. He leaves but writes a letter of explanation, especially concerning Wickham, who is in fact a wastrel and ingrate and has topped his villainies by trying to seduce Darcy's young, vulnerable and rich sister. Slowly Elizabeth comes to see that she has put too much faith in her first impressions of both men.

To cheer herself she takes a trip with her sensible aunt and uncle, the Gardiners, people in trade in London and therefore quite below Darcy in status. Assuming his absence they visit his estate in Derbyshire – Elizabeth is impressed by what she sees and understands the full consequence of Mr Darcy and his proposal. At this point he appears. Both are awkward but both have already been changed by the other. Darcy asks the Gardiners to fish on the estate, thus treating them as equals, while Elizabeth reins in her pertness. Their burgeoning love is interrupted by the news that Wickham has run away with Lydia with little intention of marrying her. Darcy leaves Elizabeth, who assumes he has rejected her now that her family is thoroughly disgraced. In fact he has gone to London to pay Wickham to marry Lydia. When Elizabeth returns home, she learns of this and understands she is still loved by Darcy. Despite strong opposition from Darcy's aunt, Lady Catherine de Burgh, the two come together, as do Jane and Bingley; from time to time Mr Bennet escapes his wife to visit both couples.

The above plot can be seen as the blueprint for the romantic novel. Lovers meet early on and then are separated by circumstances, the hostility of others or their own psychological problems. But the reader believes throughout that it is important they be united. Throughout the novel they are not physically together much and other plots set off the main love story. In their quest for a fulfilling relationship, the lovers must come to understand more about themselves. The work will mix realism and romance and educate the reader, who will be pleased to have understood the hints about a satisfying conclusion and feel brighter and more alive at the close.

What is *Pride and Prejudice* about?

Pride and Prejudice has been called the story of a manhunt. In a way, that's exactly what it is. From the perspective of Mrs Bennet, the business of life is to get her daughters married. The same can be said of Lady Lucas, mother of plain, sensible Charlotte. For the girls themselves, the choice of a husband will be the most important decision they ever make.

Pride and Prejudice, then, is about marriage – about the tensions between the ideal of romantic love and social and economic pressures; about the dangers of being imprudently swept away by passion; about the difficulty, especially acute in a civilised society with limited opportunities for intimacy, of understanding potential partners well enough to make reliable judgements about them. (An underlying theme of the novel is how little we can really know of other people.)

Opposite: Mr and Mrs Bennet , one of Hugh Thomson's famous illustrations for the 1894 edition . Others appear throughout this book.

Mr. & Mrs. Bennet

That *Pride and Prejudice* is about the fraught business of finding a husband is evident from the beginning. The justly famous opening sentence plunges us into the ironic Austen world, a world where reality is often very different from what we are told it is:

> *It is a truth universally acknowledged, that a single man in possession of a good fortune, must be in want of a wife. (1)**

The truth, of course, is that poor single women need

*Throughout this book, the numbers in brackets refer to the chapters from which quotations are taken.

THE NARRATOR OF *PRIDE AND PREJUDICE*

In many 19th-century novels the narrator is omniscient: that is, the reader takes as authoritative what is said by a voice that enters the consciousnesses of its characters and provides an overall world view. In contrast, an unreliable narrator is one who seems untrustworthy and has to be circumvented: the reader must see round what is being told. Austen's narrator in *Pride and Prejudice* is neither quite one nor the other but rather an ambiguous consciousness that mostly seems to know all while occasionally sharing the bemusement and partial knowledge of the reader and the characters. Unlike the heroine, who in conventional romance must be appealingly discreet, the rich husbands if they are not to end up lonely old maids with little to live on. And since the choice of mate must usually be made when they are little more than nubile girls, the decision is heavily influenced by parents, as the second sentence of the novel, with its sly emphasis on the word "property", brings home. When a single man arrives in a new neighbourhood, we are told, the notion is

> *so well fixed in the minds of the surrounding families, that he is considered the rightful property of some one or other of their daughters. (1)*

The mood, for much of the novel, is one of anxious

---

narrator can display wit, irony and even satirical mockery of the "good". Sometimes the narrator helps the illusion that the story is real life; at others she draws attention to the constructed nature of the fiction: "It is not the object of this work to give a description of Derbyshire..." (42)

During the novel, the narrator slowly aligns herself with Elizabeth's consciousness. Sometimes the narrator shows more knowledge than the heroine,

as with Darcy's growing love for Elizabeth; at others the narrator refuses to guide us, letting the reader share the heroine's errors, as in the case of her encounter with Wickham. In early meetings Elizabeth urges the young man on to indiscretion about the past with Darcy and she then indecorously repeats to him Darcy's words: "I do remember his boasting one day at Netherfield, of the implacability of his resentments". On short acquaintance she declares that Darcy is "disagreeable" expectation. The marriages Mr Bennet's daughters make will determine their happiness, and they start with the disadvantage of living in a world controlled by men. If this is the story of a manhunt, it is one in which the hunters are forced to be passive, constrained by the customs of the time. (It is Mr, not Mrs, Bennet who has to call on their newly arrived neighbour, Mr Bingley.) Women wait and watch. Throughout *Pride and Prejudice*, women in drawing rooms wait for men to arrive:

[Elizabeth] looked forward to their entrance as the point on which all her chance of pleasure for the evening must depend. (54)

and "ill-tempered", that "Everybody is disgusted with his pride". (16) Although both she and the reader will come to view this conversation as improper, there is no narrative placing at the time and the inattentive reader may be wrong-footed.

Likewise there is no comment on Elizabeth's avowed aim for the Netherfield ball: she intended to conquer "all that remained unsubdued of [Wickham's] heart". (18) Much later it is made clear that Wickham is no more than a typical rake and fortune–hunter, but we could know this earlier only by close reading. Through close reading we would learn of his inappropriate disclosures about his past – would a man worthy of trust traduce Darcy so openly to a woman he scarcely knows? – and we might be wary of Elizabeth's attraction to a man who, like herself, is not quite secure in status. She believes them both to be making a stand against "the mere stateliness of money and rank". (29)

The narrator does hint at

Elizabeth, under scrutiny by Miss Bingley,

> *expected at every moment that some of the gentlemen would enter the room. She wished, she feared that the master of the house might be among them. (45)*

Jane waits in London, hoping Mr Bingley will call on her. Mrs Bennet waits for a son:

> *Five daughters successively entered the world, but yet the son was to come; and Mrs Bennet, for many years after Lydia's birth, had been certain that he would. (50)*

Wickham's unreliability early on. As Susan Morgan points out, his tale is told to Elizabeth – and the reader – in the form of a sentimental story, and elicits from her the proper forms of response: "Indeed!" "Good heavens!" "How strange!" "How abominable!" (16) Elizabeth is convinced because "there was truth in his looks" (17), and as he talks Wickham becomes "handsomer than ever". (16) For her, says Morgan, "the credibility of Mr Wickham's story is inseparable from his handsome face". (This is an example of the way the book encourages us to be wary of appearances.)

The subtlety of the narrative technique in *Pride and Prejudice* enables us both to sympathise with Elizabeth and to see beyond her: here, as in all her novels, Austen gives us a sense of community; of the values and predilections and obsessions of the society in which her characters move and from which they can't escape. Her sense of "neighbourhood" is so acute that the neighbourhood almost seems to emerge as

The atmosphere of the Bennet household is determined by the Beckett-like realisation that "the period of protracted waiting", as the critic Nina Auerbach shrewdly observes, is like "a probationary period before life begins: waiting for a male is life itself". Women tend to stay still in the novel; it is the men who move, and with a few exceptions – such as Elizabeth's visit to Derbyshire – when women move it is in the wake of men.

Unsurprisingly, they are often bored and fretful and forlorn: they complain that the country is "bare of news" (7), and about "the dullness of everything". (42) "The insipidity and yet the noise; the nothingness and yet the self-importance a character in its own right. When Lydia is discovered to be married rather than ruined, for example, the narrator tells us that the neighbourhood bore the news "with decent philosophy"; it would rather have had a scandal:

> To be sure, it would have been more for the advantage of conversation had Miss Lydia Bennet come upon the town; or, as the happiest alternative, been secluded from the world, in some distant farm house. But there was much to be talked of, in marrying her; and the good-natured wishes for her well-doing, which had proceeded before from all the spiteful old ladies of Meryton, lost but little of their spirit in this change of circumstances, because with such a husband, her misery was considered certain. (50)

The summary of local gossip in such a matter-of-fact tone tells the reader the usual fate of girls such as Lydia – prostitution ("come upon the town") or of all these people!" says Miss Bingley petulantly of the (largely female) society round Netherfield. (6) Most of the first volume of the novel consists of women talking, thinking and scheming about men.

It is as if the world only becomes real when men come into it. We are given almost no details of Longbourn House, for example, until a man – Mr Collins, to whom the house is entailed – arrives; for the reader, as for its inhabitants, it seems insubstantial, almost invisible, presented to us, in Nina Auerbach's words, "in part as Mrs Bennet perceives it – as an inherently lost and already half-vanished mirage". No answer is given to Darcy's "You cannot always have been at Longbourn" (32),

---

exile (as happens to the adultress in *Mansfield Park*). The bleakness of these alternatives, and the unpleasant way they are discussed, is mitigated by the wit of the narrative voice, but they are real enough nonetheless.

The narrator's style in *Pride and Prejudice* is one of the beauties of the book. Often the style seems a lighter version of the style associated with the critic, poet and famous man of letters, Samuel Johnson (whom Austen greatly admired and called "my dear Dr Johnson").

This is a measured style of balanced syntax and frequent generalisation, relying on abstract terms such as "duty" and "good-breeding" and assuming that the reader will accept the standards such words propose.

The style could easily become sententious, but, enlivened by Austen's wit and irony, it is rarely that, and it shows the harsh realities of the world she is writing about in a palatably entertaining way. ◆

contributing to the house's impalpability or "vaporousness". As Auerbach says,

> It is men who bring domestic substance into the representation of this world... the first male to grace [the Bennets'] table is Mr Collins, and in token of the reality of male appetite, Mrs Bennet gives us the first domestic detail of Longbourn we have seen – a fish they do not have.*

It is men, too, who create whatever strength of sisterhood we see in the novel – Elizabeth's confidences, and Jane's, revolve entirely around Darcy and Bingley. "Not merely is the descriptive energy of the novel reserved for the homes the girls marry into: only the presence of suitors brings substance to the families they leave." Despite Mrs Bennet's aura of awfulness, she is, up to a point, in league with her creator as she tries to drive her daughters out of a non-home into the establishments they deserve.

For driven out they must be; the future of the family depends on it. The girls are living in a house which doesn't belong to the family, never has, and never will. And their mother has truth on her side when she expostulates to Elizabeth after she has

---

* Much later, when Bingley and Darcy dine there as prospective husbands, we are given more details about the food, and this time there is an abundance of it. ("The venison was roasted to a turn - and everyone said, they never saw so fat a haunch." (54))

turned down Mr Collins's proposal of marriage:

> *"If you take it into your head to go on refusing every offer of marriage in this way, you will never get a husband at all – and I am sure I do not know who is to maintain you when your father is dead." (20)*

Yet Elizabeth is right to turn down Mr Collins, just as, the novel suggests, Charlotte Lucas is right to accept him. *Pride and Prejudice* is a novel which values romantic love – indeed romantic love is at its heart; Darcy is easily Austen's most passionate hero. Moreover, passion can lead to great happiness, as in the story of Darcy and Elizabeth it does. But passion alone is not enough: for one thing it is rarely, in Austen's novels, fully reciprocated (Elizabeth's feelings are never quite as strong as Darcy's); for another, mutual understanding, shared interests and a balance of temperaments are more important in the making of a successful, enduring partnership. Even these are hard to achieve and most women are not as lucky as Elizabeth: they have to settle for second, or even, like Charlotte, third best. In the world Austen is writing about, marriage, for women, however inadequately based, is almost always better than the alternative.

How much is Mr Bennet to blame for his daughters' misfortunes?

Immediately after the famous first sentence, we are within a conversation: "'My dear Mr Bennet,' said his lady to him one day, 'have you heard that Netherfield Park is let at last?'"(1) We speedily learn that while Mrs Bennet has husbands for her daughters on her mind, Mr Bennet baits her for amusement, though he soon tires of the game.

When the dialogue between Mr and Mrs Bennet ends, the narrative voice provides direct comment.

ENTAILS & MARRIAGE SETTLEMENTS

The entail, now obsolescent, was a legal arrangement which usually arose from wills and tied up the future of an estate, ensuring that it couldn't be sold or divided up. Under the entail in *Pride and Prejudice*, Mr Bennet has only a life interest in Longbourn, meaning he and his family can live there while he is alive. He has no authority to dictate to whom it should pass on his death, as the arrangement decrees it should be inherited by the next male heir. Had Mr Bennet fathered a son, it would pass to him, but it cannot pass to any of his daughters. The nearest male heir, therefore, is Mr Bennet's cousin, Mr Collins. It was sometimes possible to break an entail, by challenging it in the courts, but Mr Bennet has clearly chosen not to attempt this.

A marriage settlement

This underlines what we have learnt: that Mr Bennet is "so odd a mixture of quick parts, sarcastic humour, reserve, and caprice" and his wife a woman "of mean understanding, little information, and uncertain temper" whose "business of... life" is to get her daughters married. (1) As the book goes on, we will learn that even this description is limited: it has not caught the vulgarity and irrepressibility of Mrs Bennet, nor has it pointed out that Mr Bennet, as a father of a large family, is much to be blamed for baiting his wife and ignoring the needs of his daughters. It should be his as well as his wife's "business" to think of their future.

Mr Bennet is an attractive figure. He is witty and

was a legal document guaranteeing that the bride would have a certain sum "settled" on her – in other words, that she was entitled to the interest from that money during her lifetime, and could pass it on to her children in her will. It also stated what she would be entitled to if she were widowed. A girl's marriage settlement was usually determined by her dowry (how much money she brought into the marriage). If the husband were very wealthy he might supplement this, as Mrs Bennet thought

Mr Darcy might.

Mrs Bennet came into her marriage with £4,000. If her husband should die before her, she would receive £5,000 from his personal estate, to be shared among the girls and herself. After her mother's death, Elizabeth would have only £40 a year – about what a governess earned. So Mr Collins is right when he says: "Your portion is unhappily so small." (19) When Lydia married, she was given her share of the family money and an allowance of £100 a year. ◆

funny, refreshingly refuses to conform to the stuffier forms of the time and speaks his mind. Early in the story he says to Elizabeth: "Wherever you and Jane are known, you must be respected and valued; and you will not appear to less advantage for having a couple of – or I may say, three very silly sisters". (41) He is wrong – they would and do suffer – but it is an appealing point of view.

Mr Bennet has the detachment of a playwright and part of the delight of the book is seeing social events through his eyes as well as Elizabeth's. A pessimist, he has made his peace with an inadequate world by irony and by dramatising his place in it,

AUSTEN'S FOOLS

In *Aspects of the Novel*, the novelist and critic E.M. Forster divided fictional characters into the "flat" and the "round". "Flat" characters can be quickly summed up; they exist in fixed character traits with repeated eccentricities of speech or gesture. They are usually treated satirically and may be grotesque. "Round" characters are complex, capable of surprise and contradiction, and they can change; they represent human beings in all their complexity.

In Forster's terms, Sir William Lucas is a flat character, as, of course, is Mr Collins, although the latter is given some depth with the mention of an overbearing father, restricted youth and mixed (though predominantly comic) motives for approaching the Bennet girls: "This was his plan of amends – of finding amusement in what might otherwise be painful: "For what do we live, but to make sport for our neighbours...?" (57) His habit is so ingrained that he cannot emerge from his irresponsible detachment even when the consequences may be disastrous for his family.

Since he is an intelligent man surrounded by fools, Mr Bennet suffers loneliness as well as boredom until his daughter Elizabeth is old enough to share his outlook: he then makes her a sort of substitute wife with whom he can share private jokes and whom he expects to support his opinions – as she largely does until pulled into the orbit of Mr

---

atonement – for inheriting their father's estate." (15) Austen's "fools", as Henry James called them, make up a "set of certainties against which more intricate exhibitions of pride and prejudice are measured".

Although Elizabeth declares that "intricate characters are the *most* amusing" (9), Austen loves her grotesques and gives them much space. But she also uses them to comment on her "round" characters: she allows us to see similarities between the two. For example, the first proposal of Mr Darcy has some echoes of the amusing proposal of Mr Collins; Lydia Bennet shares some traits with her sister Elizabeth – as the latter comes to realise when she watches Lydia expressing herself far too freely in the inn. She would not have been as vulgar but she accepts that the "coarseness of the sentiment" was hers. (39) Likewise, the fatuity of Mr Collins is an extreme version of the social and necessarily hypocritical manners Elizabeth and all the other sensible characters have to accept if they wish to live easily in society. ◆

Mr Collins and Mrs Bennet

Darcy. Then she realises that her father has exposed what he should have palliated. He should not, for example, have been "enjoying the scene" of his family's ill-breeding at the Netherfield ball. (18)

His heir, Mr Collins, comes to Longbourn with intentions that surely any parent would approve: marrying one of the girls so that the estate remains in their family. Mr Bennet's reaction on meeting him, however, is to think that his cousin "was as absurd as he had hoped, and he listened to him with the keenest enjoyment". (14) When he hears Mr Collins is to marry outside the family, so removing the house and estate from his wife and daughters should he die,

> *Mr Bennet's emotions were... tranquil... and such as he did experience he pronounced to be of*

*a most agreeable sort; for it gratified him, he
said, to discover that Charlotte Lucas, whom he
had been used to think tolerably sensible, was as
foolish as his wife, and more foolish than his
daughter! (23)*

Mr Bennet has failed to see Elizabeth or any of
his daughters as vulnerable young women. At one
moment he will make Elizabeth a surrogate wife to
share his adult jokes, often against her mother; at
another he reduces her to a child: he responds to
her serious warning over Lydia's wild conduct by
addressing her as "Poor little Lizzy!" and calling her
possible suitors "squeamish youths". (41) Despite
seeing through Wickham, he lets the young man
dine often at Longbourn and mingle with his girls
in "general unreserve" (24), and he watches even
Elizabeth becoming attracted to him. It is left to
her sensible aunt Gardiner to make the obvious
point that Wickham is not husband material,
however amiable.

Very late in the novel we hear of Mr Bennet's
past: how, as a landowner with an income of £2,000,
he fell for the beauty and apparent good humour
of a silly girl beneath him in rank. As a result he
lost all "respect, esteem, and confidence" as well as
the chance of domestic happiness. (42) Then,
instead of combating his wife's influence over their
children, he withdrew into his library and made
no effort to provide for their future either through

financial support or through training. The real bleakness with which he responds to Elizabeth's proposal concerning Darcy – "My child, let me not have the grief of seeing *you* unable to respect your partner in life. You know not what you are about" (59) – does not compensate for the selfishness and carelessness with which he has behaved to his family. His self-indulgent response to his own marital error is echoed in the comic rebuke in *Sense and Sensibility*, when the heroine, Elinor, muses on the ill-matched Mr Palmer:

> *His temper might perhaps be a little soured by finding, like many others of his sex, that through some unaccountable bias in favour of beauty, he was the husband of a very silly woman – but she knew that this kind of blunder was too common for any sensible man to be lastingly hurt by it.*

Wickham can elope with Lydia because he knows her father is impotent. The news of her downfall provokes "excessive distress" (46) in Mr Bennet but no practical help. He realises it "has been my own doing, and I ought to feel it", but he remains unreformed. (48) Soon he is mocking his family as usual, imagining himself in his wife's shoes giving "as much trouble as I can" or imprisoning silly Kitty as if in a gothic novel. Even the statement in which he admits his guilt is delivered for his own amusement: "Let me once in my life feel how much I have been to blame. I am not afraid of being overpowered by the impression." His habit of mind is too ingrained for change. When the catastrophe is averted he withdraws again from any paternal role and makes no remonstrance to Lydia, as Mrs Gardiner futilely tries to do.

The narrator declares that Elizabeth had "never been blind to the impropriety of her father's behaviour as a husband" and his defiance of "conjugal obligation and decorum which, in exposing his wife to the contempt of her own children, was so highly reprehensible". (42) After she has been influenced by Darcy's letter and criticism, she takes her father to task over his refusal to discipline Lydia. He jokes about her concern: Lydia "cannot grow many degrees worse, without authorising us to lock her up for the rest of her life". (41)

It is tempting to sympathise with Mr Bennet. But are we right to do so? Should we be so gentle in our response to this man who so lets down his family and so ill-prepares his daughters for the world? It is his irresponsibility, not his wife's, which enables Wickham to elope with Lydia and which threatens to blight the marriage prospects of all his daughters.

What makes Elizabeth Bennet such an engaging heroine?

Jane Austen herself called Elizabeth Bennet "as delightful a creature as ever appeared in print", a verdict endorsed by generations of readers. Unlike the passive and vulnerable protagonists of some of the conventional romances Austen read in her childhood, Elizabeth has vitality and vivacity and a cool scepticism about life. She is funnier and less snobbish than Emma Woodhouse, less priggish than Fanny Price (the most disliked of Austen's heroines), and more spirited than Elinor or Marianne in *Sense and Sensibility*. As a result it is entertaining to see most of the action of the novel through her eyes.

In *Sense and Sensibility*, the romantic Marianne cannot abide the silliness of inconsequential social chit chat; Elizabeth, sharper and more sophisticated, manages both to be tolerant of it and to distance herself. Through her we can find the empty conversations entertaining; at the same time we can listen and laugh with her.

Like all Austen's heroines, Elizabeth has a "self-created quality", as D.W. Harding puts it. She is able to develop beyond her family, in a sense to outgrow them. "Elinor Dashwood, Elizabeth Bennet, Fanny Price, Emma, Anne Elliot, are either motherless or have had to acquire standards other than those their mothers could have inculcated."

Yet while this is true, the subtlety of Austen's art in *Pride and Prejudice* is clear from the way in which Elizabeth is shown to be flawed, and to have inherited character traits from both her parents.

She has, for example, her father's slightly alarming tendency to judge society. In a bleak moment, she remarks to her sister:

> *There are few people whom I really love, and still fewer of whom I think well. The more I see of the world, the more am I dissatisfied with it; and every day confirms my belief of the inconsistency of all human characters, and of the little dependence that can be placed on the appearance of either merit or sense. (24)*

When on her visit to her friend Charlotte at Huntsford she sees Miss de Burgh and realises this is the girl Darcy is supposed to marry, she comments in her father's accents: "I like her appearance... She looks sickly and cross. – Yes, she will do for him very well. She will make him a very proper wife." (28) The romantic reader might think Elizabeth is being perverse and that her remark shows a fascination with Darcy; nonetheless it is cynical. Elizabeth has learnt the habit, useful for a disappointed, middle-aged man but not for a girl of marriageable age, of deriving humour and entertainment from socially

"Unable to utter a syllable"

awkward situations or unsatisfactory acquaintance.

When Lady Catherine de Burgh and her daughter arrive at the Collinses, Elizabeth exclaims: "and is this all... I expected at least that the pigs were got into the garden." (28) It is amusingly deflating, in the manner of Mr Bennet, a put-down for the Lucases, including Charlotte, who have maintained their awe of the great lady. But there is some vulgarity as well and we might almost hear the tone of Mrs Bennet and her favourite daughter, Lydia. Like her mother, Elizabeth at times can seem "ill-bred": to the incivility of the Bingley sisters, who exclude her as they take their walk, Elizabeth responds by naughtily citing the landscape theorist William Gilpin's remark on the picturesque quality of trios in a field – knowing the reference is to arranged cows.

When she is with Lady Catherine at Rosings, Elizabeth almost boasts of her family's lack of restraint, declaring the daughters had no governess and could, unconventionally for people of their rank, all be in society and open to marriage offers at the same time. In fact, it is unwise for five daughters all to be "out" – that is, on the marriage market – without proper coaching or restraint, and the lack of a governess or formal education, while not disadvantaging Jane and Elizabeth, has not had a good effect on the younger daughters. Here, once again, Elizabeth is not entirely unlike her mother

Opposite: Mrs Bennet, on hearing the news of Elizabeth's engagement

when the latter boasts that the countryside has sexual scandals as much as the town.

Parallels between mother and daughter also show in a passage half way through the novel when both are considering Mr Bingley's possible marriage to Jane:

> *As Elizabeth had no longer any interest of her own to pursue, she turned her attention almost entirely on her sister and Mr Bingley, and the train of agreeable reflections which her observations gave birth to, made her perhaps almost as happy as Jane. She saw her in idea settled in that very house in all the felicity which a marriage of true affection could bestow; and she felt capable, under such circumstances, of endeavouring even to like Bingley's two sisters. Her mother's thoughts she plainly saw were bent the same way, and she determined not to venture near her, lest she might hear too much. When they sat down to supper, therefore, she considered it a most unlucky perverseness which placed them within one of each other; and deeply was she vexed to find that her mother was talking to that one person (Lady Lucas) freely, openly, and of nothing else but her expectation that Jane would soon be married to Mr Bingley. It was an animating subject, and Mrs Bennet seemed incapable of fatigue while enumerating the advantages of the match. His being such a charming young man, and so rich,*

and living but three miles from them, were the first points of self-gratulation; and then it was such a comfort to think how fond the two sisters were of Jane, and to be certain that they must desire the connection as much as she could do. It was, moreover, such a promising thing for her younger daughters, as Jane's marrying so greatly must throw them in the way of other rich men; and lastly, it was so pleasant at her time of life to be able to consign her single daughters to the care of their sister, that she might not be obliged to go into company more than she liked. It was necessary to make this circumstance a matter of pleasure, because on such occasions it is the etiquette; but no one was less likely than Mrs Bennet to find comfort in staying home at any period of her life. She concluded with many good wishes that Lady Lucas might soon be equally fortunate, though evidently and triumphantly believing there was no chance of it. (18)

Austen's technique here is one with which she is much associated: free indirect speech (in which the narrator conveys what a speaker is thinking by using some of his or her characteristic words and some idiomatic turns of phrase). First, Elizabeth ponders the possibility of her sister marrying Bingley; next, she listens with growing shame as her mother talks to Mrs Lucas about it. We are given Mrs Bennet's words through her daughter's consciousness, and we see Elizabeth recognising her mother's mental and linguistic vulgarity and trying to restrain her. Yet we also see in this brilliant passage that there might be some slight resemblance between the mother and her second daughter.

It is not just that they tend to "run on" – the phrase Mrs Bennet has used earlier in the narrative to describe Elizabeth's habit of getting carried away. It is that we hear of Elizabeth's fantasy about Jane

AUSTEN'S SPIRITED HEROINES

Elizabeth Bennet is not the only witty and spirited young woman in Jane Austen's fiction. Two appear in the later novels, *Mansfield Park* and *Emma*; an earlier one is the villainous heroine of the unpublished novella, *Lady Susan*. Knowing that "Consideration and esteem as surely follow command of language as admiration waits on beauty," Lady Susan manipulates all around her with her command of different registers, from the witty and flirtatious to the sentimental and pathetic.

Emma, in the novel of the same name, is probably the heroine most like Elizabeth Bennet in Austen's published novels. Emma differs from Elizabeth Bennet in having a childlike rather than a clever, sardonic father and a silly, already married sister rather than four chattering ones at home. Consequently, Emma has not had the practice of mingled repartee and control that Elizabeth has had with her heterogeneous family. But, like Elizabeth Bennet, Emma is cleverer than those around her and prone to giving free rein to her wit, even when it is inappropriate. On one especially fraught occasion she is unable to

– having no "interest" of her own to pursue, she imagines Jane "settled in that very house, in all the felicity which a marriage of true affection could bestow" – immediately before we hear of her mother's thoughts on the same subject. (18)

Although one passage emphasises money, the other affection, both make the house central, and we might see here a foreshadowing of Elizabeth's propensity to locate her own union within a

restrain a clever remark at the expense of an old and garrulous friend, whom she rather comically accuses of being unable to ration her speech. The remark shocks the community and especially her mentor and later lover, Mr Knightley, who chastises her. Like Elizabeth Bennet, Emma learns more restraint as she moves towards the satisfactory marriage, but she too does not lose her ebullience, and she is left still incorrigibly matchmaking as she thinks of future children for herself and beloved governess, now Mrs Weston.

The other witty woman, Mary Crawford in *Mansfield Park*, is more problematic.

Mary is not the heroine of the novel. The heroine is the meek, virtuous and shy Fanny Price, accused by some critics of priggishness. Mary, Fanny's rival for the affections of her beloved cousin, Edmund, is a sophisticated woman from a louche London household. She charms Edmund with her free wit and risqué remarks, although, as an intended clergyman, he is troubled by her mockery of the church and in the end Mary loses him to the virtuous Fanny because her sexy wit shocks him into realising that she has "No reluctance, no horror, no feminine, shall I say, no modest loathings" of sexual impropriety. ◆

particular place. Concentrating on the language of these passages, Dorothy Van Ghent asks:

> What are the associations of words like "interest" and "bestow" [in Elizabeth's fantasy]? Do they belong to the same or a different basic idiom as "enumerate" and "equally fortunate" in Mrs Bennet's speech? In what way does the diction of "settled," "that very house," and "bestow," affect the connotations of "felicity" and "marriage of true affection"? Between these two sets of words is there, or is there not, the same ironic incongruity as between "rich" and "charming" in Mrs Bennet's conversation?

In this passage, Austen establishes some parity between the base desires of Mrs Bennet and the dreams of her more discerning daughter. For all their differences, they are not as dissimilar as they might seem. Elizabeth derives her energy from her mother, but she also shares her mother's pig-headedness, as is clear from her early stubbornness about Wickham and Darcy. Her sister Jane, pliant and trusting as she is – Jane has her father's placid temperament though not his wit – correctly holds a sceptical view about Wickham's attack on Darcy. Elizabeth takes no notice. She takes no notice either of Caroline Bingley, who tells her the truth early on. (It is a measure of Austen's subtlety that we often hear the truth through her unsympathetic characters.)

"Let me recommend you... as a friend, not to give implicit confidence to all [Wickham's] assertions; for as to Mr Darcy's using him ill, it is perfectly false; for, on the contrary, he has always been remarkably kind to him, though George Wickham has treated Mr Darcy in a most infamous manner."
(18)

If it is clear that Elizabeth is Mrs Bennet's daughter as much as she is Mr Bennet's, so, too, there is a resemblance to the trivial Lydia. Both she and Elizabeth – and indeed their mother – have been entranced by Wickham. Both laugh a lot – and laughter, in *Pride and Prejudice,* is a sign of sexual precociousness. At home, Mr Bennet has encouraged Elizabeth's spirited talk and given her no guidance as to behaviour outside. Partly as a result of this, she has developed a saucy flirtatiousness quite at odds with conduct-book advice and appalling to Lady Catherine. Elizabeth says of herself: "I dearly love a laugh." (11) When Miss Bingley declares Darcy a man at whom one cannot laugh, Elizabeth mocks the idea, then clarifies her own position: "I hope I never ridicule what is wise or good. Follies and nonsense, whims and inconsistencies, *do* divert me, I own, and I laugh at them whenever I can." (11) Lydia's laughter is more troubling: "You will laugh when you know where I am gone, and I cannot help laughing myself at your surprise to-morrow morning, as soon as I am missed," she tells her horrified family as she dashes off with Wickham. (47) She would in fact be facing certain ruin if her sister had not combined her laughing humour with appropriate restraint and been able to capture a powerful and rich man.

Elizabeth's laughter is very much part of her attraction for Darcy; he sees the erotic freedom of her wit, her taking charge of the dance and her laughing with his cousin in his aunt's stuffy drawing room. It fits with her equally disturbing and attractive physical energy, jumping over stiles, springing over puddles, and ending with dirty clothes and a glowing face. After her walk to Netherfield, Darcy is struck by "the brilliancy which exercise had given to her complexion". (7) Among the early contemporary readers we know about, only the writer Mary Russell Mitford dwelt on Elizabeth's overt sexuality, damning "the entire want of taste which could produce so pert, so worldly a heroine as the beloved of a man like Darcy".*

How is Darcy's love for Elizabeth conveyed?

Many more people now watch screen adaptations of *Pride and Prejudice* than read the book. One

* An indication of the way times have changed comes in Martin Amis's 2010 novel, *The Pregnant Widow,* when the hero, Keith Nearing, suggests that *Pride and Prejudice* has "but a single flaw: the absence, towards the close, of a 40-page sex scene".

Opposite: Jennifer Ehle and Colin Firth in the 1995 BBC series

consequence of this has been to change the way we think of Mr Darcy's role: before the first screen adaptation, the character most discussed was Elizabeth Bennet; now the popular reference is most often to her suitor.

Perhaps this shift of emphasis skews the novel and our interpretations, but it does respond to something that the original delivers: although we see him obliquely, mainly through Elizabeth's eyes, Darcy is the passionate centre of *Pride and Prejudice*. Had things turned out differently, Elizabeth would have lamented the loss of a rich and intelligent lover but would have moved on, especially since she had the sense not to broadcast the proposal and refusal to her neighbourhood. Darcy's disappointment would have been greater. The notorious plunge in the pool by Colin Firth as Darcy in Andrew Davies's BBC version is not in the book but the film-makers have responded to something that is there, a passion that the character only partially expresses in words.

Austen's Darcy is very much the upper class male, treated by everyone, especially young marriageable girls, with too much respect. So he is piqued by the vivacity and "easy playfulness" of Elizabeth. (6) Each misinterprets the other. Elizabeth assumes that Darcy has a "very satirical eye" and is meditating on absurdity (much like her father) when he is in fact only embarrassed, while so self-confident is Darcy that he interprets Elizabeth's sauciness as interest in himself, a desire to "bewitch" him. He sees a woman not quite "bordering on conceit and impertinence", as Miss Bingley describes her, but certainly one playing the marriage game cleverly. (10) Hence he believes she is "expecting his addresses" and is surprised at her rejection. In fact she often does with him what her father does with people: forces him into entertaining scenarios; on the dance floor she moulds herself and Darcy into the witty sparring couple of Restoration comedy.

Their early conversations are full of erotic banter; their fascination for each other and highly charged, articulate confrontations generate a remarkable, frenetic sexual energy. As Reuben Brower has pointed out in a celebrated essay, these confrontations are full of ironic dialogue, dialogue in which what each says to the other is open to multiple interpretations:

> *...soon afterwards Mr Darcy, drawing near Elizabeth, said to her –*
>
> *"Do not you feel a great inclination, Miss Bennet, to seize such an opportunity of dancing a reel?" She smiled, but made no answer. He repeated the question, with some surprise at her silence.*
>
> *"Oh!" said she, "I heard you before; but I could not immediately determine what to say in reply. You wanted me, I know, to say 'Yes', so that you might have the pleasure of despising my taste; but I always delight in overthrowing those kinds of*

schemes, and cheating a person of their premeditated contempt. I have therefore made up my mind to tell you, that I do not want to dance a reel at all - and now despise me if you dare."

"Indeed I do not dare." (10)

Here, as Brower says, we can interpret Mr Darcy's request to dance "more or less pleasantly, depending on whether we connect it with his present or past [more stand-offish] behaviour". Elizabeth's attack on Darcy and her archness have an irony beyond the irony she intends: she is teasing him, yet doing so, as the reader knows, while completely misreading his behaviour. On the other hand, it is possible to detect a variety of tones in Darcy's speeches. Elizabeth, says Brower,

ADAPTATIONS

Jane Austen's popularity outside the Academy derives in large part from adaptations, especially of *Pride and Prejudice*. These deliver a decorous and graceful, seemingly aristocratic world quite unlike our own; the Victorians saw the books as representing the genteel middle classes and were more concerned with Austen's depiction of rural communities than with stately homes. Now the camera lingers lovingly on rich material objects and décor, on lush fashions and plush grounds left resolutely undescribed by Austen.

Over the past 60 years, *Pride and Prejudice* has inspired many films and TV series. Each is different in its approach and style but all turn the work into a classic romance tale. All free it from the irony that, in the novel, sews doubts in the reader and from the ambiguities of free indirect speech and an unstable narrator. On stage and in film the dramatic interplay of dialogue and comment disappears. It is necessary only to look at the ending of the novel for this to become clear. In the book Mr Darcy is still not ready to be laughed at and his best friend remains the obedient Bingley, while Mr Bennet carries on his selfish life, unabashed and unrepentant, causing trouble to others and amusement to himself. The films, however, end with marriage ceremonies and all the filmic paraphernalia of romance.

In the novel, the dominating presence is Elizabeth, but, as the popular press's response to Colin Firth in Andrew Davies's BBC version can attest, the nation's enthusiasm was, in this production, more for the hero than for the heroine. Already in the novel Darcy is closer to a romantic ideal than any other hero in Austen (usually a rather ordinary young man), with his looks, estate and money; but on the screen the passion implied in the book is embodied and acted out through symbolic moments – such as the notorious plunge in the pool and resultant wet and clinging shirt. In the novel, Darcy, although often serious when regarding Elizabeth, smiles at her talk; in the adaptations he is a far more brooding presence, rather in the manner of a Brontë hero.

In the films the love story is accompanied by romantic music more suited to the intensity of Victorian literature than to the comedies of Austen, where, as Walter Scott remarked: "Cupid walks decorously". The films and television adaptations of *Pride and Prejudice* and the other works, together with Austen spinoffs, such as the novels of Georgette Heyer, have helped make the Regency period into the site of nostalgia for an elegant past make-believe world of romance. ◆

hears his question as expressing "premeditated contempt" and scorn of her own taste. But from Mr Darcy's next remark and the comment which follows, and from his repeating the question, and showing "some surprise", we may hear in his request a tone expressive of some interest, perhaps only gallantry, perhaps, as Elizabeth later puts it, "somewhat of a friendlier nature". We could take his "Indeed I do not dare" as pure gallantry (Elizabeth's version) or as a sign of conventional "marriage intentions" (Miss Bingley's interpretation), if it were not for the nice reservation: "He really believed, that were it not for the inferiority of her connnections, he should be in some danger." We must hear the remark as spoken with this qualification.

The brilliant ambiguity of this dialogue, with its variety of tones and possible meanings is reminiscent of the Augustan poet, Alexander Pope, at his satirical best. And similar patterns of irony recur over and over again. "Mr Darcy makes his inquiries (polite or impolite), asking with a smile (scornful or encouraging) questions that may be interpreted as pompous and condescending or gallant and well-disposed."

To take one more example: soon after the couple meet, Darcy comments on his own behaviour at the first of the Hertfordshire balls in a way which could be seen either as very smug or simply as modestly self-respecting:

"I certainly have not the talent which some people possess," said Darcy, "of conversing easily with those I have never seen before. I cannot catch their tone of conversation, or appear interested in their concerns, as I often see done." (31)

These early conversations reflect Darcy's divided state of mind. He has fallen passionately in love but is shocked by what has happened – and so strong is his passion, so obsessed with his own feelings has he become, that he fails to see the effect on the object of his passion.

He tries to repress his feelings, which grow stronger through repression, and we are left in no doubt of his mounting obsession: he "had never been so bewitched by any woman" (10); he "began to feel the danger of paying Elizabeth so much attention" (11); she "attracted him more than he liked". (12) Unlike Elizabeth with Jane, Darcy has no confidante: he cannot confide in his young sister or his best friend, whom he has persuaded out of a relationship with this same family. Indeed this persuasion can later be seen as part of his own defence against his feeling for Elizabeth. His horror at her relations makes the more touching the scene where he brings Elizabeth to meet his shy sister.

The way he swings between his passion and his desire to repress it is neatly brought out in a scene shortly before he proposes to Elizabeth for the first time. The couple are discussing whether it could be said that Charlotte Lucas is living near to her family, or far from them. Darcy says it is near, Elizabeth that it is far. (Perhaps, by stressing the nearness, Darcy is wondering whether he will be able to remove Elizabeth from the orbit of her family if he marries her.)

"The far and the near must be relative, and depend on many varying circumstances," remarks Elizabeth, at which point Darcy "drew his chair a little towards her". (32) Later in the conversation, however, he "experienced some change of feeling; he drew back his chair, took a newspaper from the table" and changed the drift of the conversation.

In that small advance and retreat, Darcy is perhaps miming out, albeit unconsciously, his uncertainty as to whether he can bring himself to cross the great social space which separates Elizabeth from himself. And it is, viewed in 19th-century terms, a great social space: Darcy, scion of one of England's great landowning families, is contemplating marriage to the daughter of a girl who, in early 19th-century terms, was far removed from his own social circle. For all her insufferable rudeness, it is by no means surprising that Lady Catherine de Burgh should find the prospect of an Elizabeth at Pemberley so appalling. ("Are the shades of Pemberley to be thus polluted?" (56)) It is impossible to understand the reality of Darcy's predicament, and the agitation of his feelings, without grasping this.

That he should worry about his feelings for Elizabeth is not only natural but rational and prudent, and Darcy's behaviour is contrasted strongly with that of Wickham, who elopes with Lydia with no thought to the consequences.

The strength of Darcy's passion is conveyed, as we have seen, by the dialogue between them, by the looks that Elizabeth misinterprets – he is always staring at her – and by the narrator's ironic, economical commentary. Charlotte Brontë's famous put-down of Jane Austen – "she ruffles her reader by nothing vehement, disturbs him by nothing profound: the Passions are perfectly unknown to her" – seems almost wilfully perverse. Sex was not a subject that an author of this period could openly discuss, but in the portrayal of Mr Darcy Austen comes as near to presenting sexual infatuation as she could within the conventions of the time. Edward Neill, in *The Politics of Jane Austen*, surely gets nearer the truth than Brontë when he describes *Pride and Prejudice* as "almost indecently erotic". He is surely right, too, in seeing Brontë's novel as owing much to *Pride and Prejudice.* "Rochester, and much else in *Jane Eyre*... seems completely parasitic on the Jane Austen officially patronised by Brontë."

Modern film and television adaptations have sought to bring out this aspect of the novel with Darcy revealing his obsession through bodily gestures and smouldering looks; the novel shows us none of this. Yet, for all its reticence and lack of visual description, it catches something the films rarely catch: the unexpected passionate intensity of the proposal, shocking in its directness:

In vain have I struggled. It will not do. My feelings will not be repressed. You must allow me to tell you how ardently I admire and love you. (34)

What makes Elizabeth change?

Elizabeth, of course, is much more shocked than the reader by Darcy's proposal. For all her sharpness, she is naïve, ignorant, and not as clever as she thinks she is. Significantly, she is first seen in the novel trimming a bonnet, in a room full of girls. In her father's eyes, she is still a child – "little Lizzy" – and he does not exclude her entirely from his dismissive view of his children as "silly and ignorant". During the novel, though the narrator slowly aligns herself with Elizabeth's consciousness, there are moments when, despite her acuteness of perception, we see her as just one in a gaggle of girls. [see p.12]

Elizabeth's naivety is brought out in an early scene when she is talking to Bingley. Complex characters are always difficult to read, she says, telling him that she "understands him perfectly":

> "You begin to comprehend me, do you?" cried
> he, turning towards her.
> "Oh! Yes – I understand you perfectly."
> "I wish I might take this for a compliment;
> but to be so easily seen through I am afraid is
> pitiful."
> "That is as it happens. It does not necessarily
> follow that a deep, intricate character is more or
> less estimable than such a one as yours."
> "Lizzy," cried her mother, "remember where
> you are, and do not run on in the wild manner
> that you are suffered to do at home."
> "I did not know before," continued Bingley
> immediately, "that you were a studier of
> character. It must be an amusing study."
> "Yes; but intricate characters are the most
> amusing. They have at least that advantage."
> "The country," said Darcy, "can in general
> supply but few subjects for such a study. In a
> country neighbourhood you move in a very
> confined and unvarying society."
> "But people themselves alter so much, that
> there is something new to be observed for ever." (9)

The behaviour of intricate characters can be
understood in different ways partly, as Reuben
Brower puts it, "because they are not always
the same people. The man we know today is a

different man tomorrow." Yet while Elizabeth may recognise this in theory, she is in practice still a long way from being a good judge of others or indeed herself, and in the light of her subsequent misreading of Darcy and her naïve trust in Wickham, her agreeing to the description of herself as a "studier of character" (9) is, of

THE REALISM OF *PRIDE AND PREJUDICE*

Austen's characters have a depth and complexity quite at odds with the sketchy way character is drawn in most early English novels. Both the Romantic poets and her contemporary female novelists, like Frances Burney and Maria Edgeworth, were happy to sacrifice realism to moral instruction. The closing words of Burney's *Cecilia*, for example – from which Austen probably lifted the title of her own novel – illustrate the moral didacticism which she so skilfully avoids. The book

also concerns a proud young man, Mortimer Delvile. He refuses to give up his family name on marriage to the heroine Cecilia, a necessity if she is to inherit a fortune from her uncle. The wise Dr Lyster comments on the situation at the end of the novel:

... remember: if to pride and prejudice you owe your miseries, so wonderfully is good and evil balanced, that to pride and prejudice you will also owe their termination.

In *Northanger Abbey*, another novel sketched out in the 1790s although published posthumously, Jane Austen mocks this habit of ending a novel with a resounding moral: "I leav it to be settled, by whomsoe▪

course, ironic. There is a shade of aptness in Mrs Bennet's rebuke.

Significantly, the title Austen chose for an early version of *Pride and Prejudice* was *First Impressions*, and the novel constantly emphasises how wrong-headed people's opinions can be. They make confident judgements about the world which they are then

---

it may concern, whether the tendency of this work be altogether to recommend parental tyranny, or reward filial disobedience."

As this underlines, Austen's approach is ironic, not didactic, and the world she creates in *Pride and Prejudice* is one in which men and women are shown to be fallible and limited.

The characters, for example, have faulty memories and their views of the past tend to be coloured by present desires. They repeat stories we know to be subtly altered. Elizabeth Bennet quotes to Wickham Darcy's words taken out of their original sparring context and infused with her own commentary. Later, when she interrogates her fond memory of Wickham, she starts to

doubt her own perceptions and comes to see the baseless quality of her growing love, even of her good opinion:

> She could see him instantly before her, in every charm of air and address; but she could remember no more substantial good than the general approbation of the neighbour-hood, and the regard which his social powers had gained him in the mess. (36)

Even Mrs Gardiner, Elizabeth's sensible aunt, manages to misremember under the influence of her desire and the need to please. Trying to align her views with Elizabeth's she becomes "confident at last that she recollected having heard Mr Fitzwilliam Darcy

51

forced to reconsider. They see and re-see. *Pride and Prejudice* has aptly been called "a drama of recognition" – literally re-cognition, in the sense that a mind can look again at something and make revisions and amendments. This is true not just of Elizabeth and Darcy but of the society, or community, to which they belong, always quick to rush to judgement.

formerly spoken of as a very proud, ill-natured boy" (25); in fact she cannot remember anything about him.

Elizabeth's limited vision, and misreading of Darcy, of course, is at the heart of the novel, but even after her visit to Pemberley she is by no means clear-sighted. Take the way she and Jane react to their wild sister Lydia's return home after her elopement with Wickham. They are guilty, here, of what the 18th-century philosopher David Hume called "projection"; they expect others to feel the same way about things as they do. So they imagine Lydia to be experiencing the same shame and guilt they would feel had they erred and been rescued. They are quite wrong, as they discover when the ebullient Lydia arrives home "untamed, unabashed, wild, noisy and fearless". (51)

The realism of *Pride and Prejudice* is based on Austen's psychological insights and the subtlety of her delineation of character. Physical particulars are of secondary importance; they are given to us only sparingly. Indeed the novel owes little to visual effects; mostly, the world Austen is writing about is left to us to imagine. There is minimal description of place, of rooms, furniture, of clothes, hair styles and even of physical appearance. Of Darcy we are told no more than that he is "tall" and "handsome". (3)

Austen instead appeals, as Kenneth Moler has put it, to the "mind's ear", relying on aural effects to

After one evening of seeing Darcy, Elizabeth thinks that "his character was decided. He was the proudest, most disagreeable man in the world." (3) Wickham is first of all "universally liked". (18) Not long afterwards, "Everybody declared that he was the wickedest young man in the world" (48), while the Bennets, having been "generally proved to be

bring her characters to life and she gives them each a distinctive verbal style. If anything, *Pride and Prejudice* suggests that physical description is not to be trusted: it is furnished most plentifully in the novel by Miss Bingley, whose commentary carries little authority. Of Elizabeth she pronounces:

> "Her face is too thin; her complexion has no brilliancy; and her features are not at all handsome. Her nose wants character; there is nothing marked in its lines. Her teeth are tolerable, but not out of the common way; and as for her eyes, which have sometimes been called so fine, I never could perceive anything extraordinary about them. They have a sharp, shrewish look". (45)

What brings the characters alive is not what we are told of their clothes, or their looks, but the way they speak. They don't declaim as they do in other novels of the period where speeches regularly go on for several pages. Instead they exchange brief ordinary remarks, not always freighted with significance. Many conversations are made up of hackneyed words and expressions, giving an illusion of a real talk. The characters interrupt each other and talk over each other, often failing to listen. Sometimes they talk at cross purposes, as in the proposal scene of Mr Collins and Elizabeth. And their world seems remarkably realistic, as has been eloquently noted by Dorothy Van Ghent:

marked out for misfortune" (55), are, a few weeks later, "pronounced to be the luckiest family in the world". But if the "problem of consciousness", in Tony Tanner's phrase, is how partially we see things, it can also, sometimes, be its "salvation",

---

Curiously and quite wonderfully, out of her restricted concern for the rational and social definition of the human performance there does arise a strong implication of the physical. Can one leave this novel without an acute sense of physical characterizations – even of the smells of cosmetic tinctures and obesity in Mrs Bennet's boudoir, or of the grampus-like erotic wallowings of the monstrous Mr Collins?

The American critic Deidre Shauna Lynch argues that in Austen's time readers were beginning to identify with fictional characters more closely than they had previously done. "Character reading," Lynch writes, "was reinvented as an occasion when readers found themselves and plumbed their own interior resources of sensibility by plumbing characters' hidden depths." Because we see the world around them through their eyes, they come to stand in for ourselves in their fictional world. They watch and observe – they read the world and we read it with them.

The extent to which Austen thought of her characters as real is evident from a letter she wrote shortly after *Pride and Prejudice* was published. She had been to a London portrait exhibition, hoping, but failing, she playfully told her sister, to fiind a portrait of Elizabeth Bennet. "I can only imagine that Mr Darcy prizes any picture of her too much to like it should be exposed to the public eye. And I can imagine too he would have that sort of feeling – that mixture of love, pride and delicacy." ◆

for it means we are at least able to change our interpretation of what we see and come to see it quite differently.

King Lear, says Tony Tanner, makes very clear the danger of clinging to a fixed belief. Lear is taken in by Goneril's and Regan's inflated rhetoric of love while failing to recognise the real thing in Cordelia's unadorned speech, and the tenacity with which he clings to his false conviction leads to disaster. "Elizabeth's error is not of the same order, of course, but it is of the same kind." Her happiness is possible because, unlike Lear, she eventually recognises her own pride and prejudice and changes her mind. "Time shall unfold what plighted cunning hides," says Cordelia before she is banished, and it does, but too late. In *Pride and Prejudice*, on the other hand, Darcy in his letter writes that, whatever Elizabeth may feel about Wickham, it "shall not prevent me from unfolding his real character". (35) In so doing, he succeeds in changing Elizabeth's view.

This changed perception of Wickham – even if some appreciation of his easy sociability and likeableness still remains – paves the way to her ultimate happiness. She has become better able to distinguish appearance from reality, to realise that Darcy is of an altogether different calibre from Wickham ("One has got all the goodness, and the other all the appearance of it" (40)). It is a theme as old as *Oedipus Rex*, says Tanner, and even if all that is involved is recognising a rake and a gentleman respectively for what they really are, in Elizabeth's society, no less than in ancient Greece, such acts of recognition are decisive in the procuring of happiness or misery.

In the course of the novel, Elizabeth, the "studier of character" (9), comes to be less sure of her first judgements and more given to introspection, more aware of how difficult it is to know anyone else. It might be argued that she throws off the authority of her father to take on that of Darcy – swapping one patriarchal authority for another – since the change begins after the perusal of his explanatory letter. But it is also a self-generated understanding. The passage in which she realises how blind she has been [see opposite] is what Virginia Woolf called "a moment of being", an epiphany or awakening to something not grasped before.

What Elizabeth has now seen is not some essential fixed self but the excessive power of self-indulgent judgement – or prejudice – within her. The moment is not the end of a journey into self-knowledge but a stage in a process of viewing herself – and of the reader viewing her. Though priding herself on her powers of observation she has in truth learnt little before this. She may have been a splendid talker, hence her appeal, but she has been a less accomplished listener. "Prejudice" is shown to be the result, in part, of her self-

How differently did everything now appear in which he was concerned!... She grew absolutely ashamed of herself. Of neither Darcy nor Wickham could she think without feeling that she had been blind, partial, prejudiced, absurd.

"How despicably have I acted!" she cried; "I, who have prided myself on my discernment! ... Had I been in love, I could not have been more wretchedly blind. But vanity, not love, has been my folly. Pleased with the preference of one, and offended by the neglect of the other, on the very beginning of our acquaintance, I have courted prepossession and ignorance, and driven reason away, where either were concerned. Till this moment I never knew myself." (36)

57

absorption. Even now, while she has begun to see more clearly, she still has much to learn; in appraising her, as in everything else, the book veers from absolute judgements.

"I meant to be uncommonly clever in taking so decided a dislike to [Mr Darcy], without any reason," she explains to Jane, although in fact she had a reason. (40) It is part of her acceptance that "my spirits might often lead me wrong". The Bennet family's bohemian manners, including her own, no longer serve. From this point onwards the possible views of Darcy tend to diminish and Elizabeth adjusts her opinion to the final one.

At this stage the reader is unaware that a similar process is occurring within the hero, as he admits at the end of the novel. Both characters reveal their integrity by being able to change and develop through setbacks: Elizabeth, initially, has good reason to find Darcy's behaviour haughty and offensive; he, given his background, can hardly help worrying about her family. But they are in most respects well suited to one another, and their love is of quite a different kind from Mr Bennet's foolish, youthful infatuation and from Lydia's fondness for Wickham which seems to derive largely from a crush on his uniform.

Like Henry James, Jane Austen associates integrity with intelligence. During the novel, Elizabeth shows herself able to behave more

Opposite: a poster for the 1940 fil

cleverly, and more wisely, than her father and to show a capacity for growth which is beyond him. "Introspection is retrospection," said Sartre, and Elizabeth is forced to think and think hard about what has happened to her. It is interesting, for example, to compare her reaction to the news of Wickham's attachment to the heiress Miss King with her later reaction to Darcy's letter. In the former case she writes to her aunt, Mrs Gardiner, claiming that the younger Bennets are more hurt than she by Wickham's defection, for they "are young in the ways of the world, and not yet open to the mortifying conviction that handsome young men must have something to live on, as well as the plain". (26) As Susan Morgan points out, this is "a terrible sentence, terrible in its distance from her feelings, its self-satisfied realism, its 'way of the world'. And what is most painful is to see Elizabeth choosing to make sense of her experience in such cold and easy terms." Here she very much descends to the level of her father.

In her response to Darcy's letter, however, she is quite different. She doesn't show that "quickness" her father has praised in her. Instead she thinks carefully about what she has learnt. And that, says Morgan, "is her victory. Understanding comes slowly, with a depth of feeling." During that long walk in the lane at Hunsford, Elizabeth offers, for the first time, "a picture of her mind at work. The neutral observer, the instant clarity, the conclusive wit, are gone."

How important is Pemberley in Elizabeth's transformation?

When Elizabeth jokingly says to Jane that she believes she can date her love for Darcy from her "first seeing his beautiful grounds at Pemberley" (59), her remark is in part ironic, in part true. It comprehends a fantasy of possession – not vulgar possession but rather an acceptance of all that such a house stands for: history, responsibility, status and beauty. Pemberley is a natural analogue of Darcy's character; it reflects the 18th-century view of the Earl of Shaftesbury, that "excellent aesthetic taste denotes an excellence of moral character".

In the film adaptations of *Pride and Prejudice*, the country house settings are part of the appeal. But if, to modern film-goers, the mansions all seem more or less equally splendid, there is an important distinction made in the novel between grand but "natural" Pemberley and modest Longbourn, between Pemberley and Netherfield which, like its owner, is pleasant but bland – the sharpest image we have of this is of a "charming prospect over that gravel walk" (9) – and between Pemberley and pretentious Rosings, which reflects Lady Catherine.

Elizabeth becomes a suitable potential chatelaine of Pemberley when she shows herself a viewer of taste. In the manner prescribed by aesthetic theoreticians of the time, she looks at the house and grounds from different perspectives; her educated appreciation comprehends the beauty and the value.* The chastened Elizabeth comes to Darcy through Pemberley: the house, the grounds, the housekeeper's discourse and his portrait. She had once seen him through eyes prejudiced by his poor opinion of herself; now, as he is expanded by his possessions, she looks through the prejudice of known approval.

She has always been fascinated by Pemberley. The very first mention of it at Netherfield caught her attention. And as she actually approaches it, "her spirits" are "in a high flutter", a word used of Marianne in *Sense and Sensibility* when sexually excited. Elizabeth is predisposed in its favour just as, after listening to Mr Collins, she is prejudiced against Rosings. The grounds of Pemberley, she decides at once, are neither "formal nor falsely adorned". (43)

The estate and house deliver power. Pemberley stands in for and embodies Elizabeth's new impression of Darcy and his attraction for her. (Darcy is absent but sometimes, as James Joyce once joked, "absence is the highest form of presence".) It is interesting that, as they tour the house, the Gardiners retain the scepticism about eulogies of people of rank that

*By the late 18th century, many large houses welcomed visitors, though on a small scale and mainly in an informal way, and discerning travellers, like the Gardiners, took advantage of this.

their niece has shown earlier; Elizabeth has her doubts too but is "impatient for more". (43) When she sees the portrait of Darcy she forces it into a relationship: she makes it fix its "eyes upon herself". The reader may question the comedy of erotic charm coming from a house; at this moment Elizabeth does not. The critic Adela Pinch sums it up neatly:

> After viewing the structure of the house we are led to admire its contents, then its grounds, and finally the personal advantages of the man himself. The train of our sympathies, that is, cause the figure of an individual to emerge in the text, personified through feeling – he is in his own elegant house: he is a man whose sense of self is constituted by his qualities, his extensive objects and, in particular, the esteem of others.

At Pemberley, Elizabeth sees Darcy controlling grateful servants, fish, trees, lakes and land. She notes unruptured order and mastery and finds them erotic. The combined images of grounds, house, discourse and painting envelop Darcy in the glamour of power, the kind of power she has earlier found disturbing when it seemed to be used to degrade her and dismiss her sister: "gentle sensations" follow from the idea that "many people's happiness were in his guardianship". (43) The position he can confer on a woman is "something". She thinks of "his regard with a deeper sentiment of gratitude than it had ever raised before".

TEN FACTS
ABOUT *PRIDE AND PREJUDICE*

1.

At 162,853 words, *Emma* is the longest of Jane Austen's six novels. The shortest, *Northanger Abbey*, is less than half that length: 77,977 words. *Pride and Prejudice* falls in between the two, at 122,685 words. *Clarissa*, written by Samuel Richardson in the 1740s, had 969,000 words.

2.

Pride and Prejudice is the most adapted of Austen's novels. There have been eight screen versions – two feature films and six television series. Five of these were BBC productions (1952, 1958, 1967, 1980 and 1995). The marketing slogan of the 1940 film, starring Greer Garson and Laurence Olivier, was "Bachelors Beware! Five Gorgeous Beauties are on a Madcap Manhunt!" Aldous Huxley co-wrote the script. Sales from the 1995 BBC series, in excess of $644m, have outstripped any of the films. When it was first released on VHS, the entire first run of 12,000 copies sold out in two hours.

3.

There have been numerous spin-offs of *Pride and Prejudice*. The most famous is *Bridget Jones's Diary*, the film of which took more than $281m. Spinoffs took a new turn in 2009 with the announcement by Elton John's Rocket Pictures of the forthcoming *Pride and Predator*, complete with an alien landing in Longbourn, the publication of *Pride and Prejudice and Zombies*, and Amanda Grange's *Mr Darcy, Vampyre*.

4.

The model for Pemberley is popularly believed to be Chatsworth, which Austen may have visited in 1811, despite the fact that Chatsworth is cited in the book as one of the "celebrated beauties" of Derbyshire, and is one of England's greatest aristocratic houses. It was used as the location for Pemberley in Joe Wright's 2005 film.

5.

Austen was encouraged by her family to write: they were her first readers. She never had a room of her own and she must often have written in the general sitting room. She was not eager for servants and visitors to know what she did; there is a story that she wrote on small sheets of paper which could easily be hidden or covered with blotting paper if anyone approached and that she was alerted to this by a creaking door which she did not wish mended. This helped persuade Virginia Woolf that "to Jane Austen there was something discreditable in writing *Pride and Prejudice*".

6.

The first edition, priced at 18 shillings was sold out within the year, and a second edition printed. A third edition was remaindered. *Pride and Prejudice* was published in the United States in 1832 as *Elizabeth Bennet or, Pride and Prejudice* and then was included in 1833 in Richard Bentley's Standard Novel series. It has been in print ever since.

7.

There are 44 letters used in the text of *Pride and Prejudice*, more than in any other of her novels – *Sense and Sensibility* has only 21. *First*

Impressions is thought by some critics to have consisted entirely of letters.

8.
Pride and Prejudice is one of only two of Jane Austen's novels in which the heroine's mother features as a major character, the other being *Sense and Sensibility*.

9.
Though never married, Austen indulged her childhood fantasies in the parish register of Steventon church where her father was rector. Once, she mischievously jotted in the specimen page of the marriage register: "The Banns of Marriage between Henry Frederick Howard Fitzwilliam of London and Jane Austen of Steventon".

10.
Rudyard Kipling wrote a short story, "The Janeites" (1924), whose epitaph was "Glory, love, and honour unto England's Jane!" In it, a group of soldiers form a shadow Masonic lodge, membership of which is based on their extensive knowledge of Austen's novels.

How deeply does Elizabeth fall under Darcy's spell?

After being impressed both by the letter and by the great estate, Elizabeth encounters Darcy himself. When he suddenly appears, crashing through the stylised images of Pemberlcy she has been contemplating, her response to him is not the old one of teasing pertness; she now feels shame at the way she must appear – a middle-class tourist on an upper-class estate accompanied by relations "in a low way, in trade", as Emma, a later Austen heroine, expresses it; a woman pursuing a man she has once rejected. She does manage a "sly" look at Darcy when she introduces the Gardiners of Cheapside, but her main response is astonishment and confusion. When Darcy and his shy sister come to the inn in their carriage, she again feels a quite unusual "discomposure". Then when she learns of Lydia's flight she trembles at the knees and bursts into tears. This display of feminine distress is appropriate. But it is clear that Elizabeth has changed; she has come to realise that life cannot always be met with wit and vivacity.

She has been preparing for the moment. When she met her sisters Kitty and Lydia unchaperoned in an inn, she fully understood the impropriety of her family's ways. Influenced by Darcy's view of them all, she has had the courage to tell her father that

Mr Bingley and Mr Darcy first meet Elizabeth: "She is tolerable, I suppose."

Lydia's visit to the militia in Brighton would be "the death warrant" of "common sense", and she no longer finds amusing her father's funny scenarios of Lydia as a lunatic public exhibit. (41) The two proposals she has received may also have helped alter her mindset. Mr Collins has mentioned her lack of fortune while Darcy has lamented her relations. The two men are poles apart, but both understand the power of men in the marriage market. So, contemplating her own and her sisters' situation, she has felt "depressed beyond anything she had ever known [before]". (36) To become a proper wife she has to control in public the ebullience – and sexiness – she shares with Lydia.

Despite definite movement in her thinking, Elizabeth remains witty and somewhat playful to the end – Jane smiles, she laughs. Elizabeth's detachment reflects her state of mind. She is appealing in the novel precisely because she is not infatuated. She feels affection, then gratitude, then love, for Darcy, but we never see her growing obsessed in the manner of the yearning Marianne of *Sense and Sensibility* or indeed Anne Elliot in *Persuasion*, whose life is dominated by lost love. The tendency of Elizabeth's mind is caught, rather bleakly, in the narrator's comment – which seems to belie the novel's huge reputation as the ultimate romance:

> *If gratitude and esteem are good foundations of affection, Elizabeth's change of sentiment will be neither improbable nor faulty. But if otherwise – if the regard springing from such sources is unreasonable or unnatural, in comparison of what is so often described as arising on a first interview with its object, and even before two words have been exchanged, – nothing can be said in her defence, except that she had given somewhat of a trial to the*

latter method in her partiality for Wickham, and
that its ill success might, perhaps, authorise her to
seek the other less interesting mode of attachment.
(46)

The truth is that while Elizabeth comes to "affection" she never falls passionately in love. Despite the common perception that *Pride and Prejudice* is Austen's most satisfying romance, the alliance between hero and heroine, if not as unequal as the one between Colonel Brandon and Marianne in *Sense and Sensibility*, has a similar lack of balance: infatuation on the man's part, gratitude on the woman's. Indeed Elizabeth's father's anxiety and her own coolness, together with the sense of mastery still clinging to Darcy, give a slight chill to the sunny end.

It has been argued that Elizabeth's capitulation in the second half of the book is total, to the extent that her relationship with Darcy turns into a "master-slave" one. Edward Neill in *The Politics of Jane Austen*, for example, thinks that from the outset Darcy "treads on Elizabeth... There is a persisting impulse to cow or crush, of Darcy as the figurehead of some male ruling-class juggernaut which resists the effort to reinscribe him as an acceptable wooer." And later, despite Elizabeth's outward defiance,

there is an inner crumpling which installs Darcy as an "interior paramour" in the disconcerting form of super-ego or censor. "Where super-ego is, there shall id be" seems to be the motto of this, at once the most chaste and the most erotic of courtship novels.*

Neill sees Austen as anticipating Freud's essay, "Family Romances", in which "the 'self-orphaning' child may seek out a local nobleman to claim kin from a sense of insecurity, and the inadequacy of its own parents". Family romance is very much in the air in *Pride and Prejudice*, with Elizabeth, in Freud's phrase, "feeling impaired" by what Neill calls her family's "malign neglect and culpable inadequacy". It is a family she must long to escape:

> a dim, foolish, meddling mother and an improvident, "absconding" father (true, he absconds, as it were, in situ... "retiring to his library"). Filling up the picture are two silly-flirt sisters (Kitty and Lydia) and one owlish pedant (Mary), while even the sweetly affectionate Jane is not entirely helpful in her monad-like determination to hear, see and speak no evil.

Neill's view of Elizabeth's surrender of independence to Darcy is an extreme one, but the conflict with her family which it supersedes is real enough. They are

---

*Maaja Stewart goes even further than Neill, claiming that Elizabeth is rendered "completely helpless": "her education in the novel is learning to accept her dependence".

not the tyrants of contemporary gothic fiction, but they serve the purpose of separating her from the hero, and sorely trying her. During the loud conversation between Mrs Bennet and Lady Lucas in Chapter 18, overheard by Darcy, Elizabeth clearly sees her mother as socially inept and ridiculously boastful; at the same time she is starting perhaps, at last, to observe herself and her sisters as needy, marriageable women, in the way Charlotte has always seen them. She never considers the option that the feminist writer Mary Wollstonecraft had taken a few years earlier when she had contemplated her inadequate family: of leaving home to become independent as a companion, then governess. This would not have been an attractive or credible path for someone as genteelly born as Elizabeth.

The Bennet family's imperfections become more and more apparent to Elizabeth under Darcy's gaze. Properly realising his passion for her, however crudely and cruelly expressed, she begins to overcompensate for her earlier poor opinion by accepting almost all his views. She acknowledges that her family's failings are more than "ridiculous". When her mother is in full flow before Darcy and Bingley, "Elizabeth's misery increased at such unnecessary, such officious attention!... at that instant she felt, that years of happiness could not make Jane or herself amends, for moments of such painful confusion." (53) Earlier she might have joined her father in seeing such scenes as amusing, but now she sees her father's behaviour as "a continual breach of conjugal obligation and decorum" which has exposed his wife "to the contempt of her own children". (42) Like a parent with an unsatisfactory child, she feels "disappointed and sorry" for her father. Darcy is superseding him as internal monitor. (41)

And yet while Elizabeth changes her views, and learns to curb her tongue, she is not, surely, transformed into the slave that Edward Neill makes of her. Her wit remains to the end, as we see in the final chapter when she echoes her earlier self: in one of their early meetings, Darcy had boasted that pride is under proper regulation when there is "a real superiority of mind" and she had "turned away to hide a smile". (11) She now notes that her powerful fiancé had not yet learnt to be laughed at. The "yet" suggests that, while Elizabeth must tread carefully, the relationship is unlikely to be as unbalanced as Neill imagines it will be. Equally, we are told that Lady Catherine is eventually asked as a guest to Pemberley, but only, the narrator stresses, because Elizabeth persuades Darcy to effect a reconciliation.

And Darcy, himself, of course, has been humbled too. When we finally have access to his innermost thoughts, as he talks to Elizabeth, he confesses to having been "tortured" by her accusation that he has behaved in an "ungentleman-like manner". (45) He has realised that he must match Elizabeth's inner qualities and that money and rank are not everything

20ᵀᴴ-CENTURY VIEWS OF AUSTEN

PRO...

❝ *Little touches of human truth, little glimpses of steady vision, little master-strokes of imagination* ❞
Henry James (1905)

❝ *Jane Austen is a mistress of much deeper emotion than appears on the surface. She stimulates us to supply what is not there* ❞ Virginia Woolf (1925)

❝ *An exquisite mastery of whatever can be mastered* ❞ Andre Gide (1929)

❝ *Miss Austen is almost unique among the novelists of her sex in being deeply and steadily concerned... as the great masculine novelists are, with the novel as a work of art* ❞ Edmund Wilson (1945)

ANTI...

❝ *...thoroughly unpleasant. English in the bad, mean, snobbish sense of the word* ❞
D.H. Lawrence (1930)

❝ *Physical violence is quite beyond Miss Austen's powers...[she is] 'feeble and ladylike'* ❞
E.M. Forster (1927)

❝ *At the height of political and industrial revolution, in a decade of formidable philosophic activity, Miss Austen composes novels almost extra-territorial to history* ❞ George Steiner (1975)

– just as Elizabeth learns that they are something. He falls in love with Elizabeth because of her lively wit and her ability to stand up to him; for all Neill's talk of an "aristocratic juggernaut" there is no hint in the text that the most spirited of Austen's heroines will ever allow herself to be crushed.

Does Austen think marriage is a good thing?

The 20th-century critic Dorothy Van Ghent sees Austen as consistently "setting up the impulsion of economic interest against those non-utilitarian interests implied by the words 'feelings' and 'love': marriage means a complex arrangement between the marrying couple and society – that is it means not only feelings but property". Edward Neill goes further. There is a "cruel" interpretation of the plot, he says, in which, since "the objection is to Darcy's 'improper pride'", Elizabeth "sees his property, becomes convinced of his propriety, and finally assures Mr Bennet that he has 'no improper pride', perhaps because his pride is merely coextensive with his property, and well grounded". In the same way, Lydia's "lack of virtue" is made to correlate with her "lack of economic concern", while the converse – the correlation of virtue with a concern for a prudent settlement – is true of Charlotte.

It is true that Jane Austen's view of marriage is

far from sentimental. Pemberley matters to Elizabeth – as it should. It is part of what she is marrying. And what she achieves, with Darcy, is less cynical than Neill suggests: she marries a man who loves her, whose pride she has softened, and who can also provide her with all the social and economic advantages she could wish for: she will be mistress of a great house, will want for nothing and will be able to shine in a greater world than that of provincial Longbourn.

The marriage of Elizabeth's friend, Charlotte, is very different; it is almost the antithesis of her own. But, as the novel makes clear, the situations of Charlotte and Elizabeth are scarcely comparable. Charlotte lacks Elizabeth's advantages. Elizabeth has been appreciated by her clever father and has learned to value – perhaps over-value – herself. She has had years of her mother's ebullient marriage plans, and in reaction has conceived an aversion to the scheming of most marriageable girls. She therefore misjudges Charlotte, who in reality is a plain "well-educated young woman of small fortune" with a family of brothers and two silly parents. (22) Without her friend's self-esteem, looks or youth, Charlotte cannot pretend to the independence that none of them, strictly speaking, truly has. Charlotte realises that women must "catch" men, that they must make the running, even if they cannot afford to be seen to do so. The worldly attitude of Charlotte becomes a foil to

Elizabeth's attractive, spirited and unworldly
self-assurance.

The man she is prepared to put up with is, as
Elizabeth tells Jane, "conceited, pompous, narrow-
minded" and "silly". (24) Mr Collins's absurdity
is caught magnificently in the elaborate way he
phrases his proposal to Elizabeth:

> *"But the fact is, that being, as I am, to inherit this*
> *estate after the death of your honoured father,*
> *(who, however, may live many years longer), I*
> *could not satisfy myself without resolving to*
> *choose a wife from among his daughters, that*
> *the loss to them might be as little as possible,*
> *when the melancholy event takes place – which,*
> *however, as I have already said, may not be for*
> *several years."(19)*

The syntax here, as Dorothy Van Ghent has noted,
serves not to express the moral and intellectual
refinement which this comic monster intends, but
"the antithesis of that refinement". If integrity
requires intelligence, as the novel suggests, then
Mr Collins has neither, and his speeches, muddled
and verbose, convey his stupidity. Language, as Van
Ghent puts it, "is the mirror of his degeneracy".

The unromantic nature of the attachment
between Mr Collins and Charlotte is conveyed to
us in a typically ironic passage. His proposal to her
is given in just two sentences:

Miss Lucas perceived him from an upper window as he walked towards the house, and instantly set out to meet him accidentally in the lane. But little had she dared to hope that so much love and eloquence awaited her there. (22)

Elizabeth's disappointment in Charlotte is acute, and the narrator tells us that it makes her doubt her old friend's "rectitude and delicacy". Charlotte appears to have "sacrificed every better feeling to worldly advantage". The critic Robert Polhemus goes far beyond even Elizabeth when he declares that Charlotte Lucas has acquiesced in "a kind of socially respectable prostitution". Mary Wollstonecraft, who echoed Daniel Defoe's view that marriage is "legal prostitution", would have agreed. In *A Vindication of the Rights of Men*, she lamented the fact that to "rise in the world", women had to "marry advantageously, and to this object their time is sacrificed, and their persons often legally prostituted".

But the book is far less judgemental. After the marriage, Elizabeth continues to project her own views on to Charlotte, and tries to re-create Charlotte more in her own image. She believes her friend is avoiding her new husband and that "home and her housekeeping, her parish and her poultry" will lose "their charms". (38) And yet Charlotte has married him in spite of her awareness of his limitations. She has done what women were so often being urged to do in 18th-century conduct books: made a virtue of necessity. The narrator tells us that Charlotte and Mr Collins agree in opinions. The Charlotte who emerges at Hunsford is not delivered as a disappointed woman. Towards the end of the novel we are told she is pregnant, so suggesting no extreme physical distaste (a fact that the films, which invariably translate Mr Collins's verbal absurdity into physical, do not contemplate).

In a controversial essay written in 1939, D.W. Harding set out to counter the view that Jane Austen wrote light, escapist romances. Her novels, he argues in "Regulated Hatred", reveal her fear and hatred of the mocked characters and of society generally. She clearly loathed Mrs Bennet and Mr Collins and the way in which economic and social institutions had such power "over the values of personal relationships". But even if it is true that Austen hated the society she lived in, and the sacrifices it required, she accepted it, as her characters do. Charlotte's decision to marry Collins is not ideal, but it is better, in the world she lives in, than the alternative: loneliness and poverty. Elizabeth believes Charlotte has abandoned her integrity but the novel, on the contrary, appears to endorse Charlotte's own view of her marriage.

Mr Collins, to be sure, was neither sensible nor agreeable; his society was irksome, and his

attachment to her must be imaginary. But still
he would be her husband. Without thinking
highly either of men or of matrimony, marriage
had always been her object; it was the only
honourable provision for well-educated young
women of small fortune, and however uncertain
of giving happiness, must be their pleasantest
preservative from want. (22)

Few girls are as lucky as Elizabeth; many more,
like Charlotte, have little choice but to marry a
man they don't love and, often, don't even respect.
It is the price they pay to escape from home – and
to stay solvent.

How radical is Jane Austen's view of society?

Austen's books, as we have seen, suggest the
emptiness of women's lives without men; indeed
throughout her completed works, women are
shown leading what Nina Auerbach calls "a
purgatorial life" together. Nowhere is this more
true than in *Sense and Sensibility*, where the four
Dashwood women are systematically stripped
of compensatory support by their mean-minded
half-brother and his grasping wife.

"Altogether, they will have five hundred a-year

between them, and what on earth can four women want for more than that? – They will live so cheap!"

Both Austen's first two novels, *Sense and Sensibility* and *Pride and Prejudice*, suggest that it is the fate of "superfluous" women to live in a vacuum. They have little real power; the power belongs to men. But Austen's recognition of this does not imply any feminist enthusiasm on her part for a world dominated by women. On the contrary, strong mothers and mother-substitutes in Jane Austen's works, like Mrs Norris in *Mansfield Park* or Lady Russell in *Persuasion*, are almost always pernicious

FRANCES BURNEY

Frances Burney's novels of manners, particularly *Evelina* (1778), *Cecilia* (1782) and *Camilla* (1796), depict the adventures of young ladies with good principles but little understanding of the "world". They enter society and learn to behave in a well-bred way and to separate the false from the genuine; in the process of being trained, they find true love, usually with the man who has been their mentor or model – and sometimes tormentor. Jane Austen uses Burney's entry-into-society plot but with more lightness and, as *Pride and Prejudice* shows, she was sceptical about the male mentor.

in their authority: female power seems effectively synonymous with power abused. Mrs Bennet's attempt to establish Jane at Netherfield, for example, is depicted almost as if it is an attack on her, even though it does, as Mrs Bennet hopes, further her cause with Bingley, while Lady Catherine is shown to be a monster of misgovernment.

Significantly, Lady Catherine is the only character other than Mrs Bennet to deplore the British legal custom of entailing estates solely through the male line and therefore cutting girls largely out of inheritance, something even the iconoclastic and undeferential Elizabeth accepts as a matter of course. For Auerbach, Lady Catherine serves as

Mr Darcy greatly influences Elizabeth but he is by no means equivalent to the faultless men who train the Burney heroines to become perfect wives, and Mr Knightley in *Emma* is not above feeling jealous and allowing his jealousy to cloud his judgement. (Something of Delvile, the hero of *Cecilia*, may be found in Darcy: both men are proud of family and rank and both worry about marrying beneath themselves.)

In her depiction of social embarrassment and the misery of inadequate and vulgar relations, Burney very much foreshadows Austen, although again her fictional situations are more extreme. And where Burney's young women are subjected to extreme experiences of social and sexual disgrace, often coming close to madness and death, Austen's heroines learn greater self-knowledge from commonplace events within the range of everyday life. ◆

an "image of the overweening matriarchate that would result could widow and daughters inherit the estate".

In her futile attempt to persuade Elizabeth to give up Darcy, Lady Catherine makes clear that her private great society runs on matriarchal principles:

"I will not be interrupted. Hear me in silence. My daughter and nephew are formed for each other. They are descended on the maternal side, from the same noble line; and, on the father's, from respectable, honourable, and ancient, though untitled families." (56)

After this homily, with its condescending reference to the paternal line, she warns Elizabeth not to "quit the sphere" in which she was brought up. Elizabeth stoutly replies:

"In marrying your nephew, I should not consider myself as quitting that sphere. He is a gentleman; I am a gentleman's daughter; so far we are equal."

"True, You are a gentleman's daughter. But who was your mother?"

This strikes Elizabeth at her most vulnerable point, throwing her back on the matriarchal world in which she has grown up and from which she longs to escape. By referring only to her father she has in effect come close to denying that she is her mother's daughter.

Lady Catherine's victory over her, however, is a hollow one. The power she thinks she has is a delusion. She leaves – "do not deceive yourself into a belief that I will ever recede" – receding, to be replaced by Darcy, who has the real power, the power that only men can bestow. (What compels Elizabeth in Darcy's portrait is what Auerbach calls "the awesomely institutionalised power of a man, a power that her own father has let fall".)

Elizabeth, however, does not dismiss the importance of rank. Despite her lack of deference to Lady Catherine, she has, from the start, a much more acute sense of its importance than her mother who, having moved from the middle class into the gentry – her father was an attorney – has the least sense of decorum. When Mr Collins wants to introduce himself to Darcy, the nephew of his patroness, Elizabeth tries to restrain him since she knows that the overture should come from the person of higher rank – Darcy is "superior in consequence". (18) (The phrase, ironically, brings Elizabeth close to Lady Catherine, who likes to see "distinction of rank preserved". (29)) Mr Collins disagrees since he feels himself the embodiment here of Lady Cathcrine, and he considers that he should even apologise for not having introduced himself earlier.

But, while Austen is sceptical of radicalism, *Pride and Prejudice* affirms the importance of change.

The idea that she might disgrace Darcy is one that Elizabeth does not accept – while Darcy, for his part, comes to realise that the woman he loves cannot be divorced from her family and that, in human terms, what she offers is not much worse than what he brings – an almost disgraced sister and an impertinent aunt. A healthy society, the novel suggests, depends on balance – on an accommodation between the established customs and traditions of the upper classes and the energy and imagination of individuals like Elizabeth.

There is an important moment when Elizabeth and the Gardiners visit Pemberley, a scene which suggests that social boundaries can be crossed. After meeting Darcy unexpectedly by the house, they are looking around the grounds when they come across him a second time, hurrying towards them. The implication here, perhaps, is that it is possible to bridge the social gap – that the gap between Elizabeth and Darcy can be closed.

Darcy aligns himself with the conservatism of Edmund Burke – endorsing the idea that "low connections" materially lessen a woman's chances of marrying well – but also with Wollstonecraft's more feminist attitude: he strongly believes in learning and the importance of books, and doesn't condemn Elizabeth for her wit or independence of thought. Similarly, Elizabeth, while valuing Darcy's connections, is not overawed by them, telling Lady Catherine that she does not consider the interests of the ruling class to be morally binding: "neither duty, nor honour, nor gratitude have any claim on me in the present instance. No principle of either would be violated by my marriage with Mr Darcy." (56) And while she does not really engage with Lady Catherine's resonant question – "Who was your mother? Who are your uncles and aunts?" (56) – it is one set of these derided uncles and aunts, the Gardiners, who become guests at Pemberley even before the engagement and are regular visitors after the wedding: "with the Gardiners, [Darcy and Elizabeth] were always on the most intimate

FEMALE EDUCATION

The 18th century worried about female wit. As Elizabeth Montagu, an 18th-century society hostess and patron of women writers, remarked, "wit in woman is apt to have bad consequences; like a sword without a scabbard, it wounds the wearer and provokes assailants." Unlike the kind of heroines who populated Shakespearean and Restoration comedy, by the late 18th and early 19th centuries, fictional heroines tended to be sweet rather than pert and, although often clever, seldom displayed verbal wit.

This attitude was compounded by the sharp rise in popularity of instruction manuals for female behaviour. These books had been current in Britain since the invention of printing, but the large number aimed at gentry and middle class girls (and their parents) was a phenomenon terms" since it was they who, "by bringing [Elizabeth] into Derbyshire, had been the means of uniting them". (63)

The ideal community, Austen suggests, allies a traditional ruling elite with a more thrusting, commercially minded middle class, which the Gardiners represent and which Mary Wollstonecraft in *A Vindication of the Rights of Woman* admired as providing a useful example for both men and women.

The alliance between the Gardiners and Darcy is secured by Elizabeth Bennet, the daughter of a landowning gentleman and lower-ranked provincial

---

of the period of the late 18th and early 19th centuries. These works, called "conduct" or "courtesy" books, preached traditional feminine values of prudence, modesty and proper dependence on fathers or husbands, and they usually stressed Christian seriousness and restraint. Concerned primarily with marriage, they advised a girl to hide any wit or learning she might possess and to avoid any improper energetic displays of the body.

James Fordyce's *Sermons to Young Women*, a conduct book first published in 1766,

was extremely popular and went through a large number of editions. In *A Vindication of the Rights of Woman* in 1792, the feminist Mary Wollstonecraft noted that the *Sermons* "have long made a part of a young woman's library". They contained, she thought, "many sensible observations" but were hopelessly sentimental and they encouraged "female meekness and artificial grace" in girls. The emphasis on appealing bodily weakness and total subservience to men appalled her and she classed Fordyce

Opposite: Mr Collins proposes to Charlotte Lucas and is accepted

woman. She challenges Darcy's narrow, complacent idea of what it is to be "well-bred"; true class, she suggests, is as much about intellectual, social and moral qualities as it is about wealth or an ancient name. Mr Gardiner is described when first introduced as "a sensible, gentlemanlike man" and Bingley's crass and affected sisters, themselves living off the profits of trade, are ridiculed for having had "difficulty in believing that a man who lived by trade, and within view of his own warehouses, could have been so well bred and agreeable". (25)

In all her books, Austen brings together people from different backgrounds and shows them

---

among "writers who have rendered women objects of pity, bordering on contempt" – a view which Elizabeth Bennet, the most outspoken heroine allowed to get her man, would probably have shared.

By the time of *Pride and Prejudice*'s publication in 1813, *Sermons* had considerably declined in popularity, so its use helps locate the novel in its moment of conception in the 1790s. But even in that decade, radical and conservative writers agreed that a more serious

education was wanted for girls than the training in accomplishments often condoned by conduct books. Mary Wollstonecraft proposed a rigorous and rational training for boys and girls together which would teach them how to think and analyse, so rendering them equal citizens rather than primarily gendered beings. She hoped that this new kind of education could determine development and character and in time bring about a society of equality and responsible liberty. Jane adjusting to one another and coming to a clearer understanding of their proper role in the world. The lower-ranked Elizabeth carries as much to Darcy as he to her; in *Mansfield Park*, Fanny, the dependent child of a sailor, becomes the moral centre of the great house and parsonage; and the socially secure Emma, through errors of judgement, learns the proper significance of her rank and the responsibility it entails. (No one in Austen learns to ignore class in the modern romantic fashion.) The old order is buttressed by being made aware of what it has lacked and it is renewed by taking into itself people who were not

Austen, too, approved serious reading and thinking but she seems to have doubted whether formal schooling of any sort could do more than stock a mind with facts, and she seems dubious about the views of her more utopian contemporaries.

In *Mansfield Park*, the strictly raised daughters of the house have a governess and can parrot many facts but grow up with no proper moral and social understanding of the world. In *Pride and Prejudice,* Jane Austen ridicules the intellectual ambition of Mary Bennet; there is no substitute for native commonsense. Elizabeth Bennet has firm principles despite a frivolous mother and no governess, but the younger children have not benefited from freedom. Self-knowledge and knowledge of the world, Austen suggests, are difficult to come by and do not result from introspection alone, nor from reading or from social interaction, but from a mingling of all of these. However, even then, any "knowing" remains partial. ◆

born into it, and learning from their thrusting and independent attitudes.

Austen's heroines, then, are agents of change: Elizabeth in *Pride and Prejudice* persuades Darcy to see the world differently, and to accept new social alliances. He can then use his power to ensure Lydia's respectability, to give his blessing to the wedding between Bingley and Jane, and to restore harmony to the family of his chosen bride. *

Mrs Bennet and her two youngest girls

* The theme of "connection" runs through the book. Wickham is said by Mrs Gardiner to be objectionable as a suitor because he offers "a connection imprudent as to fortune".(39) Elizabeth is sure that Darcy can be nothing to her after Lydia's marriage: "From such a connection she could not wonder that he should shrink." (50) Lady Catherine tells her that "connection with you must disgrace him in the eyes of everybody". (56)

What does *Pride and Prejudice* tell us about happiness?

While *Pride and Prejudice* is a novel about marriage, one of the major preoccupations of the novel is happiness and what it takes to achieve it. Elizabeth and Charlotte have very different ideas about this. Early on, when the two are talking together, Charlotte offers her own, cynical view:

> *"Happiness in marriage is entirely a matter of chance. If the dispositions of the parties are ever so well known to each other, or ever so similar beforehand, it does not advance their felicity in the least. They always continue to grow sufficiently unlike afterwards to have their share of vexation; and it is better to know as little as possible of the defects of the person with whom you are to pass your life."*
>
> *"You make me laugh, Charlotte; but it is not sound. You know it is not sound, and that you would never act in this way yourself." (6)*

But Charlotte's aspirations are not high. She accepts Mr Collins, knowing he is stupid, because it offers her a means to escape from home and to have an establishment of her own. Twenty seven and not pretty, she is living in a society which treats an old maid as a burden and a misfit. Economic anxiety makes her long only for security; she resolves to reduce herself to simplicity; the best she can hope for is a very limited form of happiness:

> *"I am not romantic... I never was. I ask only a comfortable home; and considering Mr Collins's character, connections, and situation in life, I am convinced that my chance of happiness with him is as fair, as most people can boast on entering the marriage state." (22)*

Elizabeth has higher expectations. She is shocked by Charlotte's marriage, as we have seen, and condemns her more passive sister Jane for the "want of proper resolution" which almost leads Bingley to "sacrifice his own happiness" and Jane's to the whims of others. (24) She is determined to be happy.

It is Elizabeth's liveliness and originality which win Darcy's heart. Her famous dash across the countryside to Netherfield to be with Jane in her illness is a reflection of her spontaneity, and while it is condemned by the jealous Caroline Bingley – "It [i.e. walking several miles alone and getting "above her ankles in dirt"] seems to me to show an abominable sort of conceited independence, a most country town indifference to decorum" (8) – it makes her all the more attractive to Darcy, who is struck by "the brilliancy which exercise had given to her complexion". (7)

Pride and Prejudice suggests that while determination, energy and independent-mindedness by no means guarantee happiness they make it more likely, especially when allied to the capacity to recognise error, which Elizabeth shares with Darcy:

> *She began now to comprehend that he was exactly the man, who, in disposition and talents, would most suit her. (50)*

Darcy, too, is spirited and independent-minded. He defies his aunt as Elizabeth defies her mother. His initial proposal to her may be offensive and arrogant, but unlike Mr Collins, who, as Vivien Jones says, lists "calculated and entirely impersonal criteria for a good wife", his words are an "irrepressible response to Elizabeth's individuality". He sacrifices his pride and prejudice for love, as she does hers. When Elizabeth learns about Darcy's saving of Lydia, "Her heart did whisper, that he had done it for her" (52), and her instincts are confirmed when he confesses that his main motivation was "the wish of giving happiness to you". (58) His own reward, when she agrees to marry him, is "happiness... such as he had probably never felt before". Romantic love, notes Jones, "makes individual happiness both the motivation and the goal of moral and social change".

The novel does not suggest that the happiness Darcy and Elizabeth achieve is easy, or common. There is a fairytale element about *Pride and Prejudice*; it is a version of the Cinderella story. Darcy is rich enough and grand enough to do as he likes; Elizabeth is clever and pretty. They are lucky to find one another. Most men and most women,

---

THE TITLE

Pride and Prejudice probably alluded to the close of Frances Burney's novel *Cecilia* (1782), where the difficulties of hero and heroine were "the result of PRIDE and PREJUDICE".

These abstract words draw on many 18th-century philosophical discussions about human nature. In his *Reflections on the Revolution in France*, the politician and author Edmund Burke had given dignity to the usually negative idea of "prejudice" by making it part of national identity: "we cherish [prejudices] because they are prejudices". And he wrote: "Prejudice renders a man's virtue his habit; and not a series of unconnected acts."

For most people, however, the word retained its modern meaning, of unanalysed and second-hand opinions. The philosophers David Hume and Adam Smith, meanwhile, saw "pride" as proper self-esteem which though essential they also thought detrimental when it blinded a person to his own character or, as in Elizabeth's case, it "mortified" another's. Put like this, pride and prejudice begin to sound remarkably similar as, of course, Austen's novel suggests that they are. ◆

even the independent minded, are not so fortunate.

Will Elizabeth ever be as happy as Jane?
Mrs Bennet thinks so, but Mrs Bennet equates
happiness with prosperity:

> *"Oh! my sweetest Lizzie! How rich and how
> great you will be! What pin-money, what jewels,
> what carriages you will have!... I am so pleased
> – so happy. Such a charming man! – so
> handsome! so tall!" (59)*

Elizabeth herself, however, is less sure. She says to
Jane:

> *"If you were to give me forty such men, I never
> could be so happy as you. Till I have your
> disposition, your goodness, I never can have
> your happiness." (55)*

This is born out by Mr Bennet, who, while anxious
about Elizabeth's future, has no doubts about his
eldest daughter's:

> *"Jane, I congratulate you. You will be a very
> happy woman." (55)*

She and Bingley, he goes on, have similar tempers:

> *"You are each of you so complying, that nothing
> will ever be resolved on; so easy, that every*

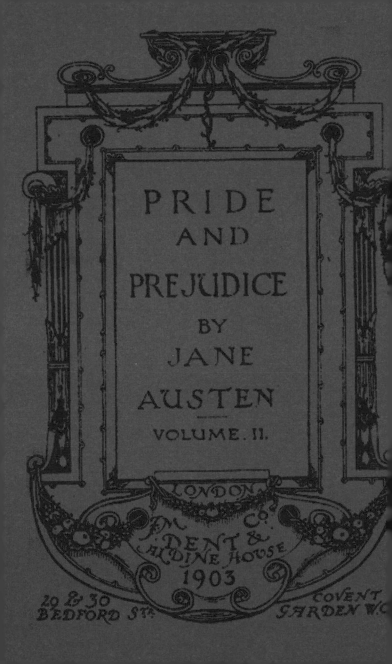

PRIDE
AND

PREJUDICE

BY
JANE

AUSTEN

VOLUME. II.

LONDON

J.M. DENT &
CO.

ALDINE HOUSE

1903

20 & 30
BEDFORD ST.

COVENT
GARDEN W.C

servant will cheat you; and so generous, that you will always exceed your income." (55)

Their relative simplicity, compared with Darcy and Elizabeth, makes their happiness seem assured. Critics have tended to be scathing about both of them. Mark Schorer, for example, calls Jane "almost limp in her goodness, and Bingley almost weak in his amiability", while Marvin Mudrick finds "something maternal, something affectionately envious, something of the nature of a schoolgirl passion" in Elizabeth's feeling for Jane, who is "gentle, sweet, forbearing, incapable of vindictiveness, incapable almost of believing ill of anyone". (35) Bingley, in this reading, is even simpler: handsome, amiable and courteous, he is led about "by the nose" by the strong-willed Darcy. Mudrick is right about this and up to a point he is right when he says that "Jane and Bingley provide us... with one of the book's primary ironies: that love is simple, straightforward, and immediate only for very simple people." Yet Jane suffers, and suffers greatly, when Bingley abandons her, and we have no reason to suppose that Bingley doesn't suffer too.

But Elizabeth and Darcy are more complex, and complex people, Elizabeth implies early in the novel, find happiness more difficult because they find each other more difficult to understand. *Pride and Prejudice*, as Reuben Brower suggests in "The

Controlling Hand", shows us that it is difficult to "know" any complex person and that "knowledge of a man like Darcy is an interpretation and a construction not a simple absolute".

Elizabeth, however, has the disposition for happiness. She looks forward with "delight" to her trip with the Gardiners; she even sets out to "enjoy" her visit to the newly married Collinses. Nothing dispirits her for long: put out when Wickham doesn't come to the Netherfield ball she quickly recovers: Elizabeth, the narrator tells us "was not made for ill-humour". (41) She lives as much as possible "in the present", she tells Darcy. Indeed so determined is she to be happy that she tries to blot out unhappy memories. Her upbringing, we surmise, was not especially happy. (She was "the least dear" to Mrs Bennet of her children.) Unlike George Eliot's Maggie Tulliver, who thinks fondly of the past – "The end of our life will have nothing in it like the beginning" – she seems not to think about her childhood at all and says to Darcy: "You must learn some of my philosophy. Think only of the past as its remembrance gives you pleasure." (58) Shortly after this, she tells Jane that she has effectively obliterated her early memories of her husband-to-be (thus erasing from her mind the good reasons she once had for disliking him):

"You know nothing of [my dislike for him]. That is all to be forgot. Perhaps I did not always love

him so well as I do now. But in such cases as these, a good memory is unpardonable. This is the last time I shall ever remember it myself." (59)

The secret of happiness, it has been said, is a good digestion and a bad memory. Elizabeth would have agreed, at least, with the second of these attributes .

How great a novel is *Pride and Prejudice*?

In *Northanger Abbey*, sketched out at about the same time as the original *Pride and Prejudice* but not published until after her death in 1818, Jane Austen provides a (slightly ironic) description of what she thought made a good novel: a good novel is a performance which has "genius, wit, and taste to recommend [it]". Mentioning some of her favourite novels by sister novelists Frances Burney and Maria Edgeworth, she calls them

> some work in which the greatest powers of the ·mind are displayed, in which the most thorough knowledge of human nature, the happiest delineation of its varieties, the liveliest effusions of wit and humour, are conveyed to the world in the best–chosen language.

Pride and Prejudice was the second Austen work to

be published (1813), the first being *Sense and Sensibility* (1811). She knew she had written something special and was aware of its worth. When she received copies of the printed work at the cottage in rural Chawton, she wrote to her sister: "I want to tell you that I have got my own darling Child from London." After mentioning a reader's reaction to her heroine, Elizabeth, she continued: "I must confess that I think her as delightful a creature as ever appeared in print, & how I shall be able to tolerate those who do not like her at least, I do not know." When her sister suggested that a few "he's and she's" might make the dialogue clearer, Jane Austen remarked that she did not write for people who "have not a great deal of ingenuity themselves".

Her enthusiasm about the book was unrestrained: as she told her sister, with her tongue in her cheek, it is "rather too light, & bright, & sparkling" – each adjective being praise itself. She pretended it needed "a long Chapter – of sense if it could be had, if not of solemn specious nonsense" to give contrast to "the playfulness & Epigrammatism of the general stile". In other words it was superior to the long, digressive and boring novels of her time – and she knew it.

She had intended the book to be distinctive. She had "lopt and cropt... successfully" her original story so as to achieve a taut, tight effect with economy in dialogue and narration. The sparkling discourse of Elizabeth and Darcy is supported by a narrative of limpid, succinct writing in which the digressions and padding she had noted in other novels are replaced by subtle changes of mood and tone. As a result, *Pride and Prejudice* has a unity to which very few other books of the period or before come near – a musical unity of chiming voices and commentary.

In his journal entry of March 14th, 1826, Sir Walter Scott lamented the author's early death. He described how he "read again, and for the third time at least, Miss Austen's very finely written novel of *Pride and Prejudice*. That young lady had a talent for describing the involvement and feelings and characters of ordinary life which is to me the most wonderful I ever met with"; he praised "the exquisite touch which renders ordinary commonplace things and characters interesting from the truth of the description and the sentiment".

Admiration was by no means unanimous. Urged to emulate Jane Austen, an irritated Charlotte Brontë dismissed *Pride and Prejudice* as passionless, as we have noted: Austen, says Brontë, "rejects even a speaking acquaintance with the stormy Sisterhood".

It is true that neither in *Pride and Prejudice* nor elsewhere in Austen's oeuvre are the upsets of life given to us as "stormy". Instead tribulations and traumas are more subtly suggested, with Austen's scorn for sentimentality and distrust of excessive emotion leading her to avoid the direct expression of overwhelming personal torment which contemporary writers such as Mary Wollstonecraft try to catch in their fictional works.

Vehement suffering and a fervent response to the world are largely absent from Austen's pages, as are a sense of social alienation and the existential loneliness of the individual human being. Her own descriptions of her lopping and cropping of *Pride and Prejudice*, and of her activity as equivalent to that of a painstaking miniaturist suggest that she was well aware that she was eliminating much from her canvas. The little works she wrote as a child are full of drunkenness, gluttony, murder and suicide, while she herself had plenty of experience of life's darker side: a disabled brother, a cousin – who had lost a husband to the guillotine – sexually attracting two other brothers, an aunt jailed as a suspect for stealing a piece of lace and therefore for a time facing death or transportation, and many painful child bearings of her sisters-in-law. And yet these aspects of life make hardly an appearance in her mature novels. Jane Austen knew the value of limits and borders; she knew what she wanted to write and how best to write it. In Dorothy Van Ghent's words "two inches of ivory" became an "elephant's tusk", a "savagely probing instrument as well as a masterpiece of refinement".

In the late 19th and 20th centuries critics tended to be divided about Austen's importance. Among her most savage critics were American male writers irritated by her narrow subject matter, her "Englishness" and her class awareness – as well as by her growing fame. Mark Twain, for example, famously lamented that it was "a great pity that they allowed her to die a natural death... Every time I read *Pride and Prejudice* I want to dig her up and beat her over the skull with her own shin-bone." (The "every time" is interesting – it is curious to keep reading a book one so dislikes.)

To Virginia Woolf, author of *Mrs Dalloway* and *To the Lighthouse*,

> Jane Austen is... a mistress of much deeper emotion than appears upon the surface... She stimulates us to supply what is not there. What she offers is, apparently, a trifle, yet is composed of something that expands in the reader's mind and endows with the most enduring form of life scenes which are outwardly trivial. Always the stress is laid upon character.

To the distinguished critic, F.R. Leavis, writing in 1940, Austen was nothing less than the inaugurator of what he called the Great Tradition of the English novel and one of a tiny handful of truly great, and morally serious, English novelists (the others being George Eliot, Henry James, Joseph Conrad and D.H. Lawrence).

But amongst Austen's novels, *Pride and*

Prejudice itself is not usually the exemplum of this praise. Marilyn Butler is one of several critics who believe that the second half of the novel is less enjoyable than the first. Marvin Mudrick also has reservations about the denouement, noting that it ends with "a conventional chase by an outraged father, a friendly uncle, and a now impeccable hero", while Reuben Brower declares that the closing events "seem to belong to a simpler world where outright judgements of good and bad or of happy and unhappy are in place. The double vision of the ironist is more rarely in evidence."

Jane Austen

HOW THE NOVEL WAS PUBLISHED

The year 1813, when *Pride and Prejudice* was first published, was a good time to be a woman writer (although it was still not entirely genteel for a *lady* to be publishing for money). Peter Garside has argued that, by the 1810s, "the publication of Jane Austen's novels was achieved not against the grain but during a period of female ascendancy" i.e. the majority of novels were written by women. Most of these were composing didactic and pious literature, melodramatic gothic novels, or nationalistic historical tales.

A writer could publish in four ways: sell the copyright and avoid further anxiety over production and sales; persuade a publisher to underwrite costs and share profits; get a subscription list to pay for publication, relying on friends, relatives and patrons; or, less commonly, publish on commission, so paying for the book production, receiving profits minus a

Other critics disagree. The feminist critics Sandra Gilbert and Susan Gubar in *The Madwoman in the Attic* (1979), for example, urge readers to read against the grain of Austen's fiction, to deconstruct, find parody and catch the rebellious, witty author beneath the decorous surface. Austen's story, they argue, may be the necessary taming of a shrew in a patriarchal culture, but it is in essence a "cover story" to express the author's own "self-division" between acquiescence and rebellious wit; it allows her to "consider her own anxiety about female assertion and expression".

---

commission, and accepting any loss. In 1811, Austen sent *Sense and Sensibility* to a London publisher, to be published on commission. It made a modest profit: she received £140. By the time she knew this, however, she had already sold the copyright of *Pride and Prejudice* for £110, admitting "I would rather have had £150". The second publication affirmed her professional status, appearing as "by the author of *Sense & Sensibility*". *Pride and Prejudice* was Austen's most popular novel; it would have brought her most profit had it been published on commission. For later novels she returned to publication on commission but none did as well as *Pride and Prejudice*.

Austen was excited by her limited success: the two first works had earned £250, which, as she wrote to a brother, "only makes me long for more". Given her small income, the money obtained from publishing – all told between £600 and £700 – was clearly important, although the sum comes nowhere near the large amounts earned by Frances Burney – £4,000 for editions of *Camilla* and *The Wanderer*. ◆

Like Elizabeth Bennet, the witty writer learns duplicitously to "exploit the evasions and reservations of feminine gentility".

While scholarly critics have argued about the power and greatness of *Pride and Prejudice*, praising its irony and techniques of dialogue, few have rated it Austen's supreme fictional achievement. Certainly it does not have the complexity of the more troubling later works such as *Mansfield Park* or *Emma*.

Yet *Pride and Prejudice* remains, and will probably always remain, the Austen novel best loved by the greatest number of readers. Although its conclusion is not as consoling as a superficial reading would suggest, it is still satisfying and – a rarity in great fiction – for the most part cheerful. With none of the dark notes which shade Austen's later works, it gives us a happy conjunction of place and person and, in contrast to Thomas Hardy's malign providence which wrecks the happiness of so many of his characters, provides a benevolent coincidence that allows its characters to be just where they ought to be at the end. The comedy, sunnier than in any of Jane Austen's other works, is mocking but never scathing. The energy and ebullience catch the joy of a youthful affection and ardour – and the excitement of an author embarking on a lifetime of writing, conscious of her talent and potential. Despite its sense of life's limitations, it is a novel which appeals both to the head – and the heart.

Exterior of the cottage at Chawton, where Austen revised Pride and Prejudice

The dining parlour at Chawton

JANE AUSTEN

A brief biography

Jane Austen wrote neither memoirs nor autobiography and she does not provide us in her novels with thinly disguised portraits of herself, an unmarried lady writer. Most information about her comes from her immediate family, primarily from the letters written to her sister Cassandra, who burnt a large number of them after Jane's death.

The critic John Wiltshire noted that we have for Jane Austen "a fantasy of access... a dream of possession". As a result, each generation makes a new image of her according to its own desire. *A Memoir of Jane Austen* (1870) by her nephew James Edward Austen Leigh created the 19th century's version: a modest, kindly and pious spinster who lived a constricted life within a family and experienced no romantic passion.

Jane Austen was born on 16 December 1775, one of eight children of George Austen, country rector in the village of Steventon, Hampshire, and Cassandra, daughter of a former fellow of Oxford's All Souls College. Jane lived her life in a web of family connections, which included on one side the rich and influential gentry and on the other clerics and an apprentice milliner. The slightly insecure family status – on the edge of the gentry – gave her an acute insight into the power of money and the subtleties of class.

Cassandra and Jane were the only girls. Apart from a handicapped boy, the brothers all had interesting careers in the church, military, navy, and banking; one was adopted by the rich Knight relations, and inherited Godmersham Park in Kent and Chawton Manor in Hampshire among other properties, all delivering an income very close to that of Mr Darcy in *Pride and Prejudice*. While her father lived, Jane had only £20 a year to spend on herself and any charities.

"Mr Darcy with him".

Mr Darcy and Mr Bingley

When Jane was in her late teens, the feminist writer Mary Wollstonecraft complained that women's lives were too restricted. Genteel girls could not become doctors or lawyers or entrepreneurs; the only real "work" society seemed to sanction was husband-hunting. (Charlotte Lucas thought marriage the "pleasantest preservative from want".) If they stayed single, women were regarded as a drain on their brothers. Jane Austen accepted the fact of female dependency on men but some of Wollstonecraft's anger is present in a character from a later novel, *Emma,* who compares her lot as potential governess to that of a slave or prostitute. Although never expressed in Wollstonecraft's feminist manner, the psychological and financial predicament of the unmarried woman is made quite clear in all the novels, including *Pride and Prejudice*.

Jane and her sisters had some brief schooling but were mainly educated through reading in their father's library and conversing with educated family members. They were all voracious readers especially in fiction. "*Our* family... are great Novel-readers & not ashamed of being so," Jane wrote in a letter to Cassandra. (In her works only the foolish characters like Mr Collins of *Pride and Prejudice* or John Thorpe of *Northanger Abbey* scorn novels.) Neither sister married, although Cassandra was engaged to a clergyman who died. Jane is known to have flirted briefly with Tom Lefroy, and when she was 26 received a proposal from a wealthy young man, Harris Bigg-Wither. She accepted, then almost immediately rejected him. (There is much speculation about romance in the hidden periods of her life but nothing is known for sure.) Throughout their lives the sisters' closest relationships were with each other.

In 1801, the Austens moved to Bath for the father's health. Little is known of the following years. Probably Jane worked on her first three novels (one of which was *First Impressions*) and also began a fourth, *The Watsons*, never completed. In 1805 her father died and the Austen women became largely dependent on Jane's brothers. They travelled between relatives until in 1809 Edward (the brother adopted by the Knights) offered his mother and sisters a free place to live in Chawton (now the Jane Austen museum), a cottage on the main road, with flower and vegetable garden and pasturage for a donkey. Jane Austen lived there for the rest of her life, making frequent trips to London and Edward's main country house at Godmersham.

At Chawton she became a professional writer and revised her three novels, turning *First Impressions* into *Pride and Prejudice*. Sadly the original versions no longer exist, and the cancelled and rewritten chapters of a late work, *Persuasion*, form the only surviving manuscript related to a completed novel. They support her brother Henry's claim that she needed "many perusals" before she was satisfied with her work. Not a writer who achieved supreme results at once, she needed to rewrite and rework to arrive at economy.

The first two published novels were originally drafted in the 1790s, the decade of the French Revolution and political unrest in Britain. Although they were somewhat revised during the Regency, Austen kept the integrity of her inspiration and there remains considerable difference between the three novels (the third early conceived one, *Northanger Abbey* was published in 1818) and the final three (*Mansfield Park*, *Emma* and *Persuasion*) composed entirely at Chawton. They are all romances concluding in marriage but the last ones leave a more troubling sense of what might have happened and of the inevitable compromises of adult life.

For most of Austen's life, England was at war with France in the French Revolutionary and Napoleonic conflicts, and something of the anxieties of war intrudes into the later novels; in *Pride and Prejudice*, started when the conflict was beginning, the only overt hint of war is the existence of soldiers in Brighton and Meryton – and the opportunities this provides for nubile girls. When *Pride and Prejudice* is adapted for the screen, it is almost invariably given the fashions and setting of the Regency, not of the 1790s. One notable example is MGM's 1940 film with Laurence Olivier, with its mid-Victorian fashions.

By 1816 Jane Austen was ill with the disease that

would kill her. Nonetheless she began a final novel, *Sanditon*, in January 1817. It was unfinished when she died on 18 July 1817 at the age of 41, possibly from Addison's disease. She was buried in Winchester where she had been taken for medical treatment.

A prettified version of the portrait painted by her sister Cassandra, assumed to be of Jane Austen

A SHORT CHRONOLOGY

1747 Samuel Richardson's *Clarissa*

1766 James Fordyce's *Sermons to Young Women*

1775 December 16th Jane Austen born in Steventon, Hampshire, to Rev. George and Cassandra Austen, the seventh of eight children, and the younger of two daughters.

1782 Frances Burney's *Cecilia*

1783-86 Attends boarding schools with her sister Cassandra in Oxford and Reading.

1787-93 Writes various short works which she would later collect in three bound notebooks now known as the *Juvenilia.* These are often exercises in parody including *Love and Freindship* [sic.], a burlesque novel of sensibility and her *History of England*, which comically satirised Oliver Goldsmith.

1789 Blake's *Songs of Experience*

1790 Burke's *Reflections on the Revolution in France*

1791 Thomas Paine's *The Rights of Man*

1792 Mary Wollstonecraft's *Vindication of the Rights of Woman*

1793 France declares war on Britain at the start of the French Revolutionary Wars. Louis XVI and Marie Antoinette executed.

1797 *First Impressions* (later rewritten as *Pride and Prejudice*) rejected for publication.

1798 Wordsworth and Coleridge: *Lyrical Ballads.*

1800 The Napoleonic Wars in Europe: France now led by Napoleon Bonaparte. Austen's brother, Francis, made a captain in the navy. He later becomes a rear admiral.

1805 Rev. George Austen dies; succeeded as rector at Steventon by his son James.

1809 Austen moves with her sister and mother to a cottage at Chawton owned by her brother Edward.

1811 *Sense and Sensibility* published. George III declared irretrievably mad, and his son made Prince Regent.

1812 Napoleon invades Russia. Britain at war with the United States.

1813 *Pride and Prejudice* published by Thomas Egerton. The first edition sold out and a second was published in November.

1814 *Mansfield Park* published.

1815 *Emma* published. Austen invited by the Prince Regent to dedicate the novel to him. It is reviewed by Sir Walter Scott in the *Quarterly Review.* Battle of Waterloo.

1817 July 18th Austen dies. In December *Northanger Abbey* and *Persuasion* published posthumously, with 1818 on the title page.

1869 James Austen Leigh's *A Memoir of Jane Austen.*

1940 First film of *Pride and Prejudice* made by MGM.

BIBLIOGRAPHY

Jane Austen's Letters, Ed. Deirdre Le Faye, OUP , 1995

Amis, Martin, "Jane Austen's World", *New Yorker* (January 8th 1996), 31-35

Brower, Reuben A, "'Light, Bright and Sparkling': Irony and Fiction in *Pride and Prejudice*" in *Fields of Light*. OUP, 1951, 164-181

Butler, Marilyn, *Jane Austen and the War of Ideas*, OUP, 1975

Duckworth, Alistair, *The Improvement of the Estate: A Study of Jane Austen's Novels*, The John Hopkins University Press, 1994

Fergus, Jan, *Jane Austen: A Literary Life*, Macmillan, 1991

Freud, Sigmund, "The Family Romance" in *The Uncanny,* Penguin, 2003

Gilbert, Sandra and Susan Gubar, "Inside the House of Fiction: Jane Austen's Tenants of Possibility" in *The Madwoman in the Attic*, Yale Nota Bene, 2000

Harding, D.W, "Regulated Hatred: An Aspect of the Work of Jane Austen" in Monica Lawlor (ed.) *Regulated Hatred and Other Essays on Jane Austen*, The Athlone Press, 1998

Honan, Park, *Jane Austen: Her Life*, Weidenfeld and Nicolson, 1987

Lascelles, Mary, *Jane Austen and Her Art*, OUP, 1939

Leavis, F.R. *The Great Tradition*, Chatto and Windus, 1948

Lynch, Deidre Shauna (ed.), *The Economy of Character: Novels, Market Culture, and the Business of Inner Meaning*, University of Chicago Press, 1998

Moler, Kenneth, *Jane Austen's Art of Allusion*, Viking, 1968

Morgan, Susan, *In the Meantime: Character and Perception in June Austen's Fiction*, University of Chicago Press, 1980

Mudrick, Marvin, *Jane Austen: Irony as Defense and Discovery*, Princeton University Press, 1952

Neill, Edward, *The Politics of Jane Austen,* Palgrave Macmillan, 1999

Polhemus, Robert, *Erotic Faith, Being in Love from Jane Austen to D.H. Lawrence*, University of Chicago Press, 1990

Stewart, Maaja, *Domestic Realities and Imperial Fictions: Jane Austen's Novels in Eighteenth Century Contexts*, University of Georgia Press, 1993

Tanner, Tony, *Jane Austen*, CUP, 1986

Tomalin, Claire, *Jane Austen: A Life*, Viking 1997

Todd, Janet (ed.), *Jane Austen in Context*, CUP, 2005

Trilling, Lionel, "Why We Read Jane Austen", *Times Literary Supplement* (March 5th 1976), 250-52

Van Ghent, Dorothy, "On Pride and Prejudice" in *The English Novel, Form and Function*, Harper Collins, 1953

Wiltshire, John, *Jane Austen and the Body*, CUP, 1992

Woolf, Virginia, "Jane Austen" in *The Common Reader*, Vintage, 2003

INDEX

First published in 2011 by
Connell Guides
Short Books
3A Exmouth House
Pine Street
London
EC1R 0JH

10 9 8 7 6 5 4 3 2 1

Picture credits:
p 11; p 24; p30; p 69; p 89; p 92; p 09 (top); p 109 (bottom); p 111; p 115
@ Jane Austen's House Museum
p 39 @ Moviestore Collection Ltd/ Alamy
p 59 @ Photos 12/ Alamy

A CIP catalogue record for this book is available from the British Library.
ISBN 978-1-907776-02-1
Design © Nathan Burton
Printed in Great Britain by Butler Tanner & Dennis Ltd

www.connellguides.com